The American Superintendent
2020 Decennial Study

The American Superintendent 2020 Decennial Study

Edited by Christopher H. Tienken

Foreword by Daniel A. Domenech

ROWMAN & LITTLEFIELD
Lanham • Boulder • New York • London

Published by Rowman & Littlefield
An imprint of The Rowman & Littlefield Publishing Group, Inc.
4501 Forbes Boulevard, Suite 200, Lanham, Maryland 20706
www.rowman.com

6 Tinworth Street, London SE11 5AL, United Kingdom

British Library Cataloguing in Publication Information Available

Library of Congress Control Number: 2020947507

ISBN: 9781475858471 (cloth : alk. paper)
ISBN: 9781475858488 (pbk. : alk. paper)
ISBN: 9781475858495 (electronic)

Contents

Illustrations

FIGURES

TABLES

Foreword

Daniel A. Domenech, executive director of AASA

Historically, public education has mirrored America's economic, political, and demographic trends. Throughout the past decade, we've seen the economy moving into the information and technology age at a rapid pace. We've also seen a steady uptick toward a diverse national demography as well as an erosion in political norms. Therefore, it is no surprise that we've had a profound impact on the role public education has when it comes to preparing students to meet the ever-increasing demands placed on them in an ever-changing society.

Today, five years past the passage of the Every Student Succeeds Act—which reestablished local school system leaders' control over academic practice and school operations—superintendents are expected now more than ever to act as a steady guide in this unprecedented sea of change.

The growing expectation of public schools to meet the needs of the whole child coupled with declining state and federal resources has caused superintendents to dramatically sharpen their expertise in a diverse array of skills. These skills include innovation, pedagogy, leadership, research methods, and finance. The move to broaden a district leader's toolbox is a must-have in order for the students living and growing in the communities they serve to turn their dreams into reality and effectively face the challenges and opportunities that lie ahead of high school graduation and beyond.

These new trends have also affected the way superintendents approach their day-to-day work. To be successful, it is now a requirement for school system leaders to know how to establish useful relationships with community members, business leaders and higher education officials, resolve conflicts between stakeholders, manage staff, engage and respond to school board members, and lead conversations about equity and inclusion, while still acting as the district's expert on curriculum and pedagogy. The work is difficult, the hours are long, and the job comes with unique challenges and difficulties. Still, superintendents come back to work, reporting high levels of job satisfaction.

In the years since the last *AASA Decennial Survey*, America has experienced an historic economic boom, marked by record lows in unemployment and record highs of economic growth. This unprecedented economy has not translated into increased state and federal resources. Instead, superintendents are still doing more with less, and using innovative solutions to fill in funding, resource, and opportunity gaps. Moreover, new and expanded movements aimed at increasing student access to private schools and for-profit charter schools continue to cause the traditional public education system to compete with varying interest over already limited resources.

In the coming years, it is undeniable that superintendents will need to continue to adapt to new and lofty expectations placed on school districts to meet the individual needs of their students, while also implementing innovative strategies that drive achievement for an increasingly diverse student population.

As the leaders and chief spokespersons of America's public school systems, superintendents have critical insights, and consequently, a responsibility to influence local, state, and federal decisions to shape the future of the nation's public schools and the students they serve. Today's superintendents are more diverse than ever before, as evidenced by the group's diverse political affiliation and range of professional experiences (e.g., teacher, principal, business leaders). In addition, we're seeing an increasing number of women aspiring to become superintendents or secure roles in education administration in their respective districts and elsewhere. The weight of school system leaders' voices and collective experiences are vital to the future of the public education system and must continue to be elevated if we're going to stay on the trajectory of continuous improvement.

The 2020 edition of the *AASA Decennial Study* is a tool to compliment this important work by collecting and analyzing the landscape of the American superintendency and marks the first time PDK International has joined us in this endeavor. As the professional organization representing more than thirteen thousand school administrators across the country, AASA, the School Superintendents Association, has a keen interest in knowing its members from their leadership characteristics and pathways to the superintendency to the challenges and opportunities they face in their daily work.

AASA thanks Joshua P. Starr, Christopher H. Tienken, Noelle Ellerson Ng, and Chris X. Rogers for their work in conducting this study. We all benefit from the time and effort these individuals devoted to data collection and analysis. AASA would like to dedicate the 2020 *Decennial Study* to Theodore J. Kowalski, an accomplished academic when it comes to the role and work of the school superintendency, whose extensive previous writings and leadership and work on previous iterations of this report made this edition possible.

This study of the American school superintendency was produced in the context of unprecedented economic, demographic, and political transitions. This unique coupling was a further catalyst for innovation and reform in education.

Change is indeed inevitable and upon us, though far from final. America's superintendents will be valuable contributors and play a pivotal role in shaping the educational experience for the next generation of students. We hope that this profile of the profession is a resource to current, former, and future superintendents, those who prepare and support superintendents, and any participant involved in the dialogue for education reform, innovation, and change.

Preface

Executive Summary

This book is an extension of national decennial studies of the American school superintendent that began in 1923. The research was conducted in late 2019 and early 2020. The results are presented in various ways throughout the study, ranging from aggregate findings to two- and three-level crosstabs that disaggregate data by eight different enrollment categories. Just as findings from previous decennial studies suggested, the various job-related happenings of superintendents are not always homogeneous. They can be influenced by a multitude of factors such as district enrollment, demographic characteristics of the superintendents, and characteristics of the students and communities they serve.

This section provides an initial overview of results from the 2020 study and how some of them compare to those of the 2010 decennial study. These results are not intended to provide a complete picture of the data that were collected or the results presented in this book. More comprehensive results and interpretations can be found in the specific chapters of the study.

2020 CHARACTERISTICS OF SUPERINTENDENTS
AND THEIR EMPLOYING DISTRICTS

- The modal superintendent was a married, white (91.38%) male, who had prior experience as a principal, with two–eight years of experience being a superintendent.
- The percentage of female superintendents increased slightly from 2010 when it was 24.1% to 26.68% in in 2020. The percentage of women in the top leadership position in education is well above the 5.4% of S&P 500 companies led by a woman. Only 5% of the Russell 3000 companies have a woman in the top position.
- In terms of political affiliation, superintendents remained a diverse group, with approximately 31% identifying as democrat, 33% republican, and 32% independent.
- Approximately 59% of the respondents said they planned on being a superintendent in the next five years. This represented an increase compared to 51% of the respondents in 2010.
- Almost 34% of superintendents specified they would be retired within the next five years compared to 50% of superintendents in 2010.

- As in 2010, about 3% (2.71%) of the respondents in this study were employed in very large districts in 2020, whereas 11.76% were employed in districts with enrollments of 300 or less, representing a slight increase from 9% in 2010.
- The racial/ethnic diversity of districts in which superintendents worked increased since 2010. Only 34% of respondents worked in districts in which less than 5% of the students were non-white compared to almost 50% in 2010. The percentage of respondents employed in districts with high racial diversity (i.e., more than 50% non-white students) remained at 15%.
- Most superintendents, 80.58%, worked in districts in which more than 25% of the students were eligible for free or reduced price lunches, with 40.50% working in districts in which more than 50% of the students were eligible for free or reduced lunches.
- Approximately 52% of respondents had two–eight years of experience as a superintendent.
- Almost three-fourths (70.02%) of rural districts are led by white men, and 22.37% are led by white women. In comparison, 1.67% and 0.76% of rural school districts are led by black or African American men and black or African American women, respectively.
- Most urban school districts were led by white men (40%) followed by those led by white women (22.86%). Black or African American men led 12.86% of urban school districts, and black or African American women lead 8.57% of urban school districts. The urban districts led by Hispanic/Latinx men (7.14%) and women (4.29%) represent positive increases from previous years.

CAREER PATHWAYS AND EXPERIENCES

- Superintendents are moving into the position at earlier ages than previously reported. The majority of respondents (57%) were superintendent by the time they were 45 compared to only 49.5% of superintendents in 2010.
- 45.75% of respondents were between the ages of 41–50 when they were hired for their first superintendency and almost a third, 31.82%, were 40-years-old or younger.
- Most superintendents continued to follow the traditional career pathway to the superintendency with 96% of respondents having been a classroom teacher and 84.43% having served as a building principal. Similar to 2010, approximately 53% had at least one year of experience as an assistant principal.
- More than half (62%) of superintendents had between 5–12 years of classroom teaching experience and for almost all of the respondents (97%) those classroom teaching experiences came in a traditional public school.
- The persons most influential in helping the respondents become superintendents were other superintendents, followed by a spouse or relative.
- Superintendents reported that they were satisfied (43%) or very satisfied (49%) with their job.
- More than half of the superintendents (51.4%) indicated they would *definitely* choose to be a superintendent again if they started their career over, followed by 29% who indicated they would *probably* choose to be a superintendent again.
- Approximately 67% of respondents were hired for their first superintendent position in a district different than the one in which they had originally worked.
- Almost 39% respondents served as superintendent in more than one district.

CURRENT WORK OF SUPERINTENDENTS

- Superintendents responded that issues related to finance (45%), personnel management (41%), conflict management (37%), and superintendent/board member relations (35%) consumed most of their time.
- Job-related stress (61%), excessive time requirements (51%), and social media issues (40%) constituted the three largest problems for superintendents' current positions.
- More than half (55%) of superintendents felt *very great* or *considerable* stress in their positions compared to only 8% who felt *little stress* or *no stress*.
- Superintendents believed their greatest strengths were leading and managing personnel effectively, fostering a positive district/school climate, and relating effectively with the school board.
- Superintendents wanted to improve their skills in the areas of school improvement, finance, curriculum and instruction, and school safety.
- More than half (68%) of superintendents rated themselves *very effective* in the area of enhancing the perception of the district, whereas only 29% rated themselves as *very effective* in the area of social emotional learning.
- About half of superintendents responded that it was *important* to lead conversations about race and 40% felt it *very important.*
- Most superintendents (80%) indicated they were *very well prepared* or *sufficiently prepared* to lead conversations about race.
- Of the superintendents of color, 50% who identified as black or African American reported they were *very well prepared* to lead conversations about race, whereas 40% of superintendents who identified as Hispanic/Latinx reported being *very well prepared.*
- Only about 20% of white superintendents reported being *very well prepared* to lead conversations about race and an equal percentage noted being *not at all prepared* to lead such conversations; the highest percentage of *not at all prepared* of any racial group.
- The majority of superintendents (77%) stated they were the ones who led discussions related to equity in their districts.

PROFESSIONAL LEARNING OF SUPERINTENDENTS

- Approximately 44% of the respondents held a terminal degree in 2020 compared to 45% in 2010 and 2000. More than a third, 35.31%, held an Ed.D. and 9% held a Ph.D. in 2020.
- The majority of the degrees received beyond the B.A. were in the areas of Education Leadership (52.67%) and Education Administration and Supervision (34.16%).
- Almost three-quarters of respondents (72.68%) stated they were more likely to read education-related articles written with practitioners in mind compared to just 8% who indicated they were more likely to read original research reports.
- Only 9.82% of respondents indicated they engaged the services of an executive coach before becoming a superintendent.
- More than half of the respondents (54.87%) indicated their academic preparation was *good* and 24.09% indicated it was *excellent*, almost identical to the 78.7% of respondents in 2010 who stated their preparation was either *good* or *excellent.*
- The majority (80%) of superintendents indicated their professors in their superintendent preparation programs were *good* or *excellent*, almost exactly the same as the results from 2010 (81.1%).

Preface

- Similar to the 2010 results, superintendents were most likely to have attended continuing education provided by state superintendent associations, regional superintendent or administrator associations, and AASA.
- Superintendents responded that the most likely future topics for their professional learning were continuous improvement (40%), law/legal issues (31%), school safety and crisis management (29%), finance and budget planning (24%), and school reform/improvement (22%). In 2010, the continuing education topics identified as having the greatest value were law/legal issues, finance personnel management, school reform/improvement, superintendent-board relations, and school-community relations.
- Almost all superintendents (96%) held membership in state superintendent associations and 71% were members of AASA.

COMMUNITY RELATIONS

- Almost all (95%) of superintendents felt *Supported* or *Very supported* by their communities.
- Nearly half (45%) of superintendents felt *Very supported* by their communities and an equal amount (45%) felt *Very supported* by the largest non-white minority group in the district.
- Less than 5% of superintendents did not feel *Very supported* or *Somewhat supported* by their communities.
- Approximately half (51%) of superintendents indicated that the largest racial/ethnic minority group in the district has concerns that differ from the concerns of the racial/ethnic majority in the district.
- Less than half (41%) of superintendents engage the community in planning or advisory activities on a monthly basis, but 80% of superintendents indicated they actively seek minority group involvement when they do include the community in planning or advisory activities.
- Almost all (96%) superintendents responded they were actively involved in the communities in which they worked.
- Issues related to extracurricular activities generated the most political action among groups in 48% of the superintendents' districts, followed by funding requests (41%), and school facility development or changes (36%).
- Respondents who maintained social media accounts focused on Twitter (74%) and Facebook (74%).
- More than half of the respondents (67%) indicated they had someone in the district who was responsible for monitoring social media accounts related to the district and 67% indicated that the district encouraged principals and teachers to maintain social media accounts to communicate with parents and students.
- About a quarter (23%) of superintendents stated they maintained a social media account but rarely checked it compared to 20% who stated they posted or responded to something daily.

Acknowledgments

Theodore Creighton, professor emeritus, Virginia Tech University
Daniel Domenech, AASA executive director
Noelle Ellerson Ng, AASA associate executive director, Policy and Advocacy
Samuel Fancera, assistant professor, William Paterson University
Denver Fowler, professor, Franklin University
LaToya Goffney, superintendent, Aldine Independent School District
Jason B. Harris, superintendent, Morrisville School District
Edward Manuszak, superintendent, Dundee Community Schools
Joanne Marien, core clinical faculty, Manahattanville College
Robert McCord, professor in residence, AASA
Kenneth Mitchell, associate professor, Manhattanville College
John Puglisi, superintendent, Rio School District
Angelica Ramsey, superintendent, Pleasant Valley School District
Joan Richardson, director, 2019 PDK Poll
Christian Rogers, policy analyst, AASA
Lavetta Ross, assistant principal, Freehold Regional High School District
Joshua Starr, CEO, PDK International

Chapter One

The Evolution of the American School Superintendent

Christopher H. Tienken

In most cases, the person who occupies the position of superintendent is expected to be both a jack and a master of all trades. Federal and state accountability mandates coupled with multiple and sometimes conflicting aspirations and desires of the local community require superintendents to possess a large and nimble skill set. Superintendents must be able to assume multiple roles within the organization to accomplish the varied goals and objectives. Kowalski, McCord, Petersen, Young, and Ellerson (2010) identify five distinct roles for the superintendent: (1) superintendent as teacher-scholar, (2) superintendent as statesman, (3) superintendent as communicator, (4) superintendent as business manager, and (5) superintendent as applied social scientist. Each role requires creative and competent application of a pantheon of knowledge, skills, and dispositions.

The fluid nature of the work of the superintendent and the need to possess and effectively apply a mixture of abilities within quickly changing roles can increase stress levels, not unlike other professions. Renzulli (2019) identifies the ten most stressful professions in the United States: (1) enlisted military personnel, (2) firefighter, (3) airline pilot, (4) police officer, (5) broadcaster, (6) event coordinator, (7) news reporter, (8) public relations executive, (9) senior corporate executive, and (10) taxi driver.

SKILLS, DISPOSITIONS, AND RESPONSIBILITIES

Although *public school superintendent* did not make the list of the ten most stressful jobs, this does not mean that the position is not stressful. If you compare the requirements and performance expectations listed for the job of public school superintendent with those of the ten most stressful jobs, you will find some commonalities. Below is a brief excerpt from the job description of a superintendent in a Kansas school district that lists the minimum requirements:

> **Skills** are required to perform multiple, highly complex, technical tasks with a need to occasionally upgrade skills in order to meet changing job conditions. Specific skill-based competencies required to satisfactorily perform the functions of the job include developing and administering budgets; operating standard office equipment including utilizing pertinent software applications;

planning and managing multiple projects; preparing and maintaining accurate records; and train-ing, developing, and supervising staff.

Knowledge is required to perform algebra and/or geometry; review and interpret highly tech-nical information, write technical materials, and/or speak persuasively to implement desired ac-tions; and analyze situations to define issues and draw conclusions. Specific knowledge-based competencies required to satisfactorily perform the functions of the job include pertinent codes, policies, regulations and/or laws; current trends and practices in public educational; education code; principles of employee development and management; project development, goal attain-ment, and time management; and principles of conflict resolution.

Ability is required to schedule a significant number of activities, meetings, and/or events; often gather, collate, and/or classify data; and consider a number of factors when using equipment. Flexibility is required to work with others in a wide variety of circumstances; analyze data utilizing a variety of complex processes; and operate equipment using a variety of standardized methods. Ability is also required to work with a significant diversity of individuals and/or groups; work with data of widely varied types and/or purposes; and utilize a variety of job-related equipment. Inde-pendent problem solving is required to analyze issues and create action plans. Problem solving with data frequently requires independent interpretation of guidelines; and problem solving with equipment is moderate. Specific ability-based competencies required to satisfactorily perform the functions of the job include adapting to changing work priorities; dealing with frequent and sustained interruptions; developing and maintaining positive working relationships; facilitating communication between persons with divergent positions; implementing change; maintaining con-fidentiality; meeting deadlines and schedules; providing direction and leadership; and setting pri-orities.

A job description from a North Dakota school district included forty-one "performance re-sponsibilities" within ten broad categories: (1) relationship with the board of education; (2) recruitment/retention of staff; (3) supervision of licensed and non-licensed staff; (4) identifica-tion and implementation of board policy needs; (5) financial management skills; (6) educa-tional leadership; (7) relationship with students and parents; (8) relationship with community; (9) effective records management; and (10) supervision of building, grounds, transportation, and student safety. It is easy to identify characteristics of a police officer, broadcaster, event coordinator, news reporter, public relations executive, and senior corporate executive packed into the North Dakota position.

It appears from the job descriptions and responsibilities that superintendents are expected to be masters of all trades and not just a *jack*. It also appears that any person who meets the requirements for the superintendent position will also qualify for many of the top-ten stressful jobs.

A nonscientific survey of superintendent job descriptions from states across the country suggests that the requirements from the Kansas and North Dakota school districts are repre-sentative of the requirements from other districts in other states. In short, the role of superin-tendent is multifaceted, ever changing, rewarding, and stressful.

Although the current roles and responsibilities of the superintendent might seem overly burdensome or even extreme to some people, they make sense within a historical context of the superintendent position and the characteristics of the people who first occupied that posi-tion. An understanding of the historical context can help one better comprehend the evolution of the superintendency and the current state of the profession.

THE SCHOOL MASTER

It is usually easier to understand the themes and plot of a story when one starts from the beginning. The genesis of the superintendency began in colonial Boston. Boston Latin School is considered to be the first public school in the United States. The school was established on April 23, 1635, only 15 years after the founding of the Plymouth Colony, 5 years after the founding of the Massachusetts Bay Colony in Boston, and 141 years before the signing of the Declaration of Independence. The school was publicly funded and provided free education to boys, whereas girls attended school at home—if they attended school at all.

Aside from being the first organized school in the American colonies, Boston Latin School is also famous for educating five signers of the Declaration of Independence: John Hancock, Samuel Adams, Benjamin Franklin, Robert Treat Paine, and William Hooper. The school remained single sex until 1972 when it became coeducational. The school continues to educate students today (Boston Latin School Association, 2017).

Philemon Pormort was appointed the first *master* of the school, also known as the *schoolmaster*, or *headmaster*, on February 13, 1635. The school was publicly funded and Pormort ran it in his home. As such, the one-room schoolhouse was born. Pormort was born in 1602, in Grimsby, Lincolnshire, England, and arrived in the Massachusetts Bay Colony in 1634. Because of the untimely death of his first wife, he was married twice, and had a total of nine children.

Although Pormort's career pathway to schoolmaster and preparation is unknown, the town fathers who appointed him must have believed he possessed the skills and dispositions necessary to lead and manage the day-to-day functions of education in colonial Boston. Pormort died in 1679; that same year Europeans first saw the headwaters of the Mississippi River, in what is now Minnesota, and New Hampshire became a county within the Massachusetts Bay Colony. The leadership provided by Pormort created the foundation for what is now America's oldest continuously operating school.

THE BEGINNINGS OF THE SUPERINTENDENCY

Boston Latin School was modeled after the Free Grammar School of Boston, England. The school curriculum focused on the humanities and religion. Latin and Greek were important subjects of the day, so Pormort must have held skills in each, or at least understood how to deliver instruction for each language. The school eventually became a pipeline to Harvard University, established a year later, in 1636. The initial job description, derived from the historical statement about Pormort's appointment, included "teaching and nurturing of the children with us" (Boston Latin School Association, 2017).

Pormort's job responsibilities increased to include supervision of staff when the town fathers hired an assistant teacher, Daniel Maude, officially known as the "usher" of the school. Although Pormort did not have the title of superintendent, it appears from the historical records that his roles and responsibilities share a genealogical branch with the modern superintendent. He was responsible for the facilities (his home), the curriculum, instruction, supervision and management of staff, general organization and scheduling of the school, maintaining fiscal responsibility, reporting to the town fathers, and most likely some type of formal and informal community relations.

Pormort undoubtedly engaged in some form of personal professional learning, otherwise he probably would not have effectively administered the school. According to the historical record, Pormort earned an unknown salary plus an extra fifty British pounds a year, raised by wealthy townspeople, and payment for the house. Maude was paid an unknown salary plus an extra thirty pounds a year (Boston Latin School, 2017).

Growing Need for Schools and School Leaders

The colony of Massachusetts passed a law in 1647, known as the *Old Deluder Satan Act*, about twelve years after Boston Latin School first opened. The act required the establishment of schools in towns with fifty or more families. The act also required that the town hire a schoolmaster to teach all children to read and write. Furthermore, towns of a hundred or more families were required to have a functioning Latin Grammar School, like Boston Latin School. The value and need for the public school was recognized early on in the colonies. One reason for passage of the act was to ensure that people could read the Bible in order not to be fooled into sin by Satan (Ward, Waller, Trent, Erskine, Sherman, and Van Doren, 1907). The Bible became the first official textbook of public schools in the colony.

FORMALIZING THE SUPERINTENDENT

The Buffalo School District, in Buffalo, New York, was created via legislation in 1837 and became the first city in New York to enact legislation to develop a formal school district. The Buffalo School District is credited with the creation and appointment of the nation's first superintendent (Brunner, Grogan, and Björk, 2002, as cited in Kowolski et al., 2010). The city of Buffalo itself was officially incorporated in 1832, so the legislation of a formal school system less than decade after incorporation seems to be progressive thinking on the part of city leaders. The village of Buffalo founded its first formal school in the winter of 1807, with Hiram Hanchett as the first teacher.

Exactly thirty years after founding its first school, the Buffalo City Council created the official position of superintendent in 1837, approximately two hundred years after Philemon Pormort was first appointed the head of Boston Latin School. The position of superintendent was created as a response to the concern of the residents in Buffalo that the growing city needed a system of schools, not just a collection of schools operating independently. The existing rag-tag arrangement of schoolhouses and niche private schools created inefficiencies and resulted in overall ineffectiveness and inequity. The town leaders wanted to create a systemic approach to educating the city's youth, and they also saw the need for a central leader for the new system; thus they created the formal position of Superintendent of Schools.

OLIVER GRAY STEELE: AMERICA'S FIRST SUPERINTENDENT?

Oliver Gray Steele is recognized as being the first superintendent of the Buffalo School District and the first to hold the official title in the United States (Brunner, Grogan, and Björk, 2002, as cited in Kowolski et al., 2010). Steele's obituary stated that he was appointed to the office of the superintendent in 1837; however, Smith (1884) listed him as superintendent as of 1838 and again in 1839 in the *History of the City of Buffalo and Erie County: With Biographic Sketches of Some of Its Prominent Men and Pioneers.*

The confusion in the historical record may be due to a time lapse between the actual appointment of Steele and his assuming the formal position. It should be noted that Mr. R. W. Haskins was the Buffalo Common Committee Council on Schools' original choice to be superintendent. Haskins served only several months because of his frustration with the rigid structure of the position; this lack of flexibility interfered with his ability to make progress with organizing and managing the fledgling school district. The Common Committee of Buffalo then appointed Mr. N. B. Sprague, but Sprague also resigned after a short time, citing the same issues that drove Haskins to resign. Haskins and Sprague made recommendations for changes to the position of superintendent to give it more autonomy and formal power. Those changes were incorporated into a revision of the position Steele assumed in 1838.

Smith (1884) observed the good fortune of Steele's appointment upon his reflection of the growth of the Buffalo School District:

> This appointment was a most opportune one for the future good of the schools of Buffalo. Mr. Steele immediately made himself thoroughly familiar with the schools as they then existed, and his report of the situation in which he found them reveals clearly their utter inefficiency as educational institutions. (p. 315)

Steele immediately set out to gather data and create a strategic plan for the future of the Buffalo School District. He completed a map of the various neighborhood boundaries and possible enrollment zones within the district. Then he collected available data on the efficiency and effectiveness of the existing schools and the educational needs of the city. He presented his report and recommended a plan to reorganize the school district in 1838.

Based on revisions to the structure, roles, and responsibilities of the position of superintendent made from the earlier recommendations of Haskins and Sprague, Steele now enjoyed wider latitude to lead and manage the district. Implementation of his plans for the reorganization and growth of the school district came down to him and his colleague, who initially solicited him for the position of superintendent: Judge Hall.

Steele's original proposal for the creation of a formal school district included a small tuition for students to cover any costs that exceeded the funding provided by the state. He made an amendment to his plan in 1839 that provided for free public school to all children within the enrollment boundaries of Buffalo. The city instituted a local municipal property tax to augment state funding.

The Work of the First Superintendent

The historical record of Steele's influence on education in Buffalo and the region of Erie County indicates he had a profound impact. Smith (1884) wrote that the Buffalo School District had become a model system, due in large part to the foundation created by Steele:

> There is now in the city of Buffalo an admirable and ample school system, comprising over a hundred different institutions, public and private, which has grown up with the place under the fostering care and unselfish labors of many of her most public spirited men and women. (p. 310)

The Buffalo School District had two departments, or levels of schooling, at the time of Steele's appointment in 1837–1838: primary and grammar. Steele oversaw both departments upon his appointment (Weed, 2001). The enrollment at the time of Steele's appointment was 179 students and within one year the enrollment increased to approximately 1,500 students (United States Department of the Interior and National Park Service, 2016).

At Steele's request, Buffalo city leaders encouraged enrollment in the schools by making it free for all students under age sixteen in 1838. The schools were funded through a system of local taxation and state funding. Steele facilitated the growth of the district by creating fifteen enrollment zones within Buffalo. Students were assigned to various schools based on their enrollment zone, known then as *districts*. Buffalo is recognized as one of the first cities to offer free public education to all resident children under the system developed by Steele (United States Department of the Interior and National Park Service, 2016). Similar systems of enrollment zones and local taxation continue today in cities and towns across the country.

Leading a Vision

The expanding district of Buffalo added a high school department in 1848. The first two high schools were first housed within existing elementary schools. The high school enrollment increased so much that by 1851 the district had to purchase a building—a local mansion—for the sole purpose of creating a stand-alone high school. The repurposed mansion became the Central High School of Buffalo and remained as the only high school until 1897 when a second high school was opened, followed by a third several years later (Weed, 2001).

Steele understood that an effective education required effective facilities and an organized system for facility development and management. He immediately set out with a building campaign to secure the future of the Buffalo School District. The first new school built under Steele was located on Church Street, in district 8 of the city. A tax was levied on that district and the building was erected. The city already owned the land, but residents were previously unable to agree on a building until Steele was able to facilitate a successful proposal through a community relations campaign. The school appears to have been successful, as it was reported that enrollment rose quickly, forcing an addition to be made to the building.

Steele continued to get other buildings approved in 1838 and 1839, initiating a building boom to accommodate the growing enrollment. Steele facilitated the construction of six buildings over the two-year period of his first term as superintendent. Of course building projects are rarely conducted without controversy and complaints, and Steele's plans were not immune to either. For instance, some residents in district 8 were upset at the increased taxes, the size of the school building, and its appearance. There were reports that some people thought it too extravagant for a school. The dissatisfaction seems to have reached a crescendo at the end of 1839; Steele was not reappointed to another term of superintendent in 1840, although it is unknown how much the building campaign affected the decision not to reappointment him.

Four superintendents managed the Buffalo School District over the next five years until Steele was called upon once again and appointed to serve a new one-year term in 1845. Although additional properties and existing homes were purchased by the school district between 1840 and 1845, there had been no new buildings constructed since Steele completed his first term in the position. Steele was able to facilitate the construction of another new school building during his second time in the position and facilitated the approval of another school that was finished in 1846.

Steele left the superintendent position for the second time in 1846 but returned for a third and final appointment in 1851. He initiated a night school during his final appointment to provide additional education opportunities for the city's residents. During Steele's multiple appointments as superintendent, the district added ten school buildings, and he became known as the "Father of the Public Schools of Buffalo" (Emerson, 1899, p. 6). By the end of 1851, when Steele stepped down, the enrollment stood at 6,368 students and 94 fulltime teachers (Smith, 1884).

Community Service

Although Oliver Steele ended his career as a superintendent after the 1851 school year, he did not end his commitment to public service and the students of Buffalo. Like many current superintendents, Steele was active in his community. He was appointed to the first board of the Buffalo Fire Commissioners in 1857 to oversee the all-volunteer fire department. Under his leadership, the city subsequently purchased the first steam fire engine in 1859. He was elected as the Erie County Supervisor in 1858 (Find a Grave, 2019) and was able to influence decisions within the entire county that included Buffalo.

Steele helped organize the Buffalo City Cemetery in 1864 and was elected vice president of the board of trustees. He was part of a group of residents who felt it important that Buffalo have a cemetery befitting a city of Buffalo's status and that the cemetery be held in public hands, not corporate interests. Steele helped raise the money necessary to initially purchase over two hundred acres of land through the sale of $50,000 worth of bonds (Smith, 1884, p. 511).

In 1871 Oliver Steele was appointed president of the board of trustees for the Buffalo Normal School. The Normal School was a state-sponsored teacher training school operated under the joint direction of the superintendent of public instruction of New York and a local Buffalo board of trustees. The Normal School included a School of Practice. The School of Practice was a Buffalo public school where teacher candidates from the Normal School could practice their craft. Some might call it a *professional development school* today. Graduates of the Buffalo Normal School were certified to teach anywhere in New York (Smith, 1884, pp. 322–23). Oliver Steele continued to be active in the community into his seventies serving as president of the executive committee of the Buffalo State College and acting as curator of the Buffalo Fine Arts Academy, a member of the loan and finance committee of the Erie County Savings Bank, and real estate commissioner of the Mechanics' Society (Find a Grave, 2019).

Historical Context in Which Steele Served

The tasks accomplished by Steele seem even more impressive when one considers the historical context in which he worked. Martin Van Buren was the U.S. president the year Oliver Steele became superintendent. Van Buren is best known for putting forth a proposal that favored states' rights to decide on slavery. Van Buren's proposal ultimately led to some of the conditions that brought about the Civil War, a war that Steele and his family lived through. Texas was not yet a state and New York was a "free state" along with other northeast states. Texas and Florida became *slave states* in 1845 at the start of Steele's second appointment as superintendent of schools.

George Armstrong Custer was born in 1839, during Steele's second year as superintendent. Custer would die in the Battle of Little Big Horn thirty-seven years later. The slave revolt aboard the Amistad occurred approximately two weeks before Steele opened schools for the new academic year of 1839. That same year, the Trail of Tears took place, the largest relocation of the Cherokee Nation, based on the Indian removal act of 1830 signed by President Andrew Jackson.

The steel plow had only been invented in 1837 and the sewing machine was still five years away. High school science classes would one day incorporate the knowledge that all living things were made up of cells, a proposal that arrived in 1839. Steele might have been the first superintendent to see someone ride a rear-wheel bicycle to school, as it was invented in 1839. The light bulb did not exist and electricity in homes was still forty years away when Steele became superintendent, making night activities at the schools even more challenging.

Steele's secretaries did not have the advantage of the typewriter when Steele was appointed as superintendent. At night, he and his staff worked by gaslight, oil lamp, or candlelight and had to write everything out longhand. Steele was not able to advertise school closings because of inclement weather via the radio because Marconi had not yet invented it. The calculator was not in service, so Steele undoubtedly did all his accounting and figuring longhand or on an abacus.

Oliver Gray Steele Remembered

Smith (1884) captured the importance of education to democracy and an informed citizenry when he wrote,

> The wise policy of the American people in the early establishment of ample education facilities as fast as the country has been settled and children have needed instruction is acknowledged as one of the strongest elements of her growth as and prosperity as well as the promoter of a high degree of general intelligence among the masses. (p. 309)

Oliver Gray Steele played an important role in the establishment of the position of superintendent in the modern school district and the development of democracy. He created many organizational structures in Buffalo that brought a free public education to all students within the city limits. His influence on the structure of public school and the superintendency can still be seen today.

Steele's obituary described a leader who was selfless, humble, and driven, with the ability to envision things that did not yet exist but were necessary, and to shepherd that vision in ways that were democratic and effective. He was noted as "not an ambitious man, he did not seek either preferment or notoriety, but his tastes, attributes, and forces of character were such that he naturally found place and influence where work was to be done for the educational, benevolent, and other ends conducive to the public good" (*Buffalo Morning Express*, 1879).

Career Pathways

Steele's obituary from the *Buffalo Morning Express* provided a brief, yet fitting overview of his productive life and pathway to the superintendent. Oliver Gray Steele was born in Connecticut on December 16, 1805, to Oliver and Sarah Steele. The Steele family was one of the oldest families in Connecticut with ties to the first secretary of the Connecticut colony. Steele attended formal schooling only up to the age of twelve; he then became an apprentice to a bookbinder in Norwich, Connecticut at the age of fifteen. He moved to Buffalo in search of work in 1827 and was initially employed by H. R. Haskins, the original choice to be Buffalo's first superintendent of schools. Haskins paid Steele five dollars a week plus board. Steele worked for Haskins for three years until he went into business for himself as a bookseller and bookbinder (*Buffalo Morning Express*, 1879, p. 4). Steele married Sarah Hull in 1831; they had five children and nine grandchildren. Mrs. Steele predeceased Mr. Steele in 1875.

Steele was active in the economic and civic arenas of Buffalo. He moved to Buffalo in 1827 and was deeply involved in the civic and economic life of the city prior to becoming superintendent. He worked as the manager of the Buffalo Gaslight Company and was president of the Buffalo Waterworks. He planned the Buffalo sewer system that is still in use to this day (Emerson, 1899). He developed and worked to pass legislation that created the school district in 1837 (United States Department of the Interior and National Park Service, 2016). Steele was also an original trustee of the Mutual Insurance Company of Buffalo. He was an active member of the Buffalo Library Lyceum from its inception in 1832 and gave talks and lectures on various topics of the day.

Oliver Gray Steele was a member of the board of managers of the Young Men's Association and the Firemen's Benevolent Association in 1837. The Young Men's Association was dedicated to the "mutual improvement in literature and science" (Smith, 1884, p. 532). The association amassed more than 2,700 books in its first year, and its library was said to have been well used. The purpose of the Firemen's Benevolent Association was for "accumulating a fund for the relief of indigent and disabled firemen and their families" (Smith, 1884, p. 518).

Steele was part of a group of citizens who organized the first Buffalo Historical Society in 1862. He was elected treasurer of the society and served in the role until 1870, and then again for a final year in 1872. Steele was then elected president of the Buffalo Historical Society in 1874 for a one-year term (Smith, 1884).

Steele served in different capacities within the Buffalo government during and after his work as superintendent. He was the supervisor of the 10th ward in 1839, a councilman of the 4th ward in 1841 and 1842, ran for mayor but lost in 1844, and returned as a councilman of the 4th ward in 1847 (Smith, 1884, pp. 132,1 36–38). Oliver Gray Steele passed away on November 11, 1879, at the age of seventy-four.

Closing Remarks

Oliver Steele unknowingly created the foundation for today's superintendent. His accomplishments portray him as an effective superintendent who possessed the required skills and responsibilities listed in current job descriptions for the position. Although his story is not well known, the example he set in Buffalo appears to have transcended time and provided the roots for the growth of current-day superintendents.

The historical record indicates that Steele operated in all the role conceptions identified by Kowolski et al. (2010): (1) superintendent as teacher-scholar, (2) superintendent as statesman, (3) superintendent as communicator, (4) superintendent as business manager, and (5) superintendent as applied social scientist. His legacy stands as a testament to what the position of superintendent can signify in a community and the impact a superintendent can make.

Almost every decade, the American Association of School Administrators (AASA) conducts a comprehensive and scholarly study of the American school superintendent. This project serves to profile, document, and offer important analyses of changing demographics, professional learning, career preparation, current work contexts, and emerging issues facing superintendents. This study tells the story of the current cadre of superintendents, over 180 years removed from Oliver G. Steele, yet following his path while blazing their own.

Chapter 2 provides an outline of the methodology used to conduct the 2020 study. Chapters 3–7 present the current state of the American superintendent in five areas: (1) characteristics of superintendents and their districts, (2) career pathways, (3) current work, (4) professional learning, and (5) community relations.

REFERENCES

Boston Latin School Association. (2017). "BLS History." Retrieved from https://www.bls.org/apps/pages/index.jsp?uREC_ID=206116&type=d.

Brunner, C. C., Grogan, M., and Björk, L. (2002). "Shifts in the Discourse Defining the Superintendency: Historical and Current Foundations of the Position." In J. Murphy (Ed.), *The Educational Leadership Challenge: Redefining Leadership for the 21st Century* (pp. 211–238). Chicago: University of Chicago Press.

Buffalo Morning Express. (1879, Nov. 12). "Obituary: Oliver Gray Steele." Retrieved from https://www.newspapers.com/clip/25715977/oliver_g_steele_obituary/.

Emerson, H. P. (1899). *Schools of Buffalo: A Souvenir History and Description of the Public Schools of Buffalo.* Buffalo, NY: Ida C. Wood. Retrieved from https://archive.org/stream/schoolsofbuffalo00wood/schoolsofbuffalo00wood_djvu.txt.

Find a Grave. (2019). "Memorial Page for Oliver Gray Steele." Retrieved from https://www.findagrave.com/memorial/46266427/oliver-gray-steele#source.

Kowalski, T. J., McCord, R. S., Petersen, G. J, Young, I. P., and Ellerson, N. M. (2010). *The American School Superintendent: 2010 Decennial Study.* Lanham, MD: Rowman & Littlefield.

Renzulli, K. A. (2019, March 7). "The Most Stressful Job in America Pays $26,802: Here Are the Other Nine." *CNBC.* https://www.cnbc.com/2019/03/07/the-most-stressful-jobs-in-america.html.

Smith, H. P. (1884). *History of the City of Buffalo and Erie County: With Biographic Sketches of Some of Its Prominent Men and Pioneers. Volume II.* Syracuse, NY: D. Mason & Co. Retrieved from https://archive.org/stream/historyofcityofb02smit?ref=ol#page/n9/mode/2up/search/steele.

U.S. Department of the Interior and National Park Service. (2016). Buffalo Public School #24. Retrieved from https://www.nps.gov/nr/feature/places/pdfs/16000840.pdf.

Ward, A. W., Waller, A. R., Trent, W. P., Erskine, J., Sherman, S. P., and Van Doren, C. (1907). *The Cambridge History of English and American Literature: An Encyclopedia in Eighteen Volumes.* New York: G. P. Putnam's Sons; Cambridge, England: University Press.

Weed, G. M. (2001). *School Days of Yesterday: Buffalo Public School History.* Buffalo, NY: Buffalo Board of Education.

Chapter Two

Design and Methods

Christopher H. Tienken

This study marks the tenth decennial study conducted on the state of the American superinten-dent. The project served to profile, document, and offer valuable analyses of the changing demographics related to who attains the position of superintendent in America's public schools, the demographic makeup of school districts, superintendent professional preparation, and their ongoing training. The project examined the evolving role of the superintendent, important issues such as equity, and all facets of community relations.

The primary purpose of the study was to describe the current state of the American superintendent in five areas. The results help decision makers understand demographic trends, the changing roles and responsibilities of the superintendent, career pathways, professional preparation, and relationships with the larger community. Results from the study are regularly used for policy making at the state and national levels, as well as lobbying efforts.

The 2020 study continues the tradition of research on the superintendent that began almost a hundred years ago in 1923. Since then, the study has been repeated almost every ten years, except during the period of 1933–1952, prior to World War II and up through the start of the Korean conflict. The Department of Superintendence, a former division of the National Education Association (NEA), sponsored the early studies. The American Association of School Administrators (AASA) began to cosponsor studies with NEA in 1952 and again in 1960. By 1971 AASA was the sole sponsor of the study. The 2020 study features collaboration between AASA and PDK International with AASA being the sole financial sponsor. Daniel Domenech was the executive director of AASA and Joshua Starr was the executive director of PDK International at the time of the study. Table 2.1 presents a chronological list of the studies conducted.

The results of past decennial studies have been disseminated as reports and in other for-mats. This study, likes it predecessor *The American School Superintendent: 2010 Decennial Study,* is published in book format through Rowman and Littlefield and select results have been presented at various AASA sponsored events and distributed via the AASA website, PDK International, and other outlets.

DESIGN

This descriptive study used a mixed-methods approach. The primary data source was derived from a seventy-six-question survey of superintendent perceptions of their position. The ques-

Table 2.1.   Chronological List of Studies of the Superintendent

Year	Title	Authors
1923	*The Status of the Superintendent in 1923*	Charles E. Chadsey
1933	*Educational Leadership*	Not listed
1952	*The American School Superintendency* (30th yearbook)	Not listed
1960	*Profile of the School Superintendent*	Not listed
1971	*The American School Superintendent*	Stephen J. Knezevich
1982	*The American School Superintendent*	Luvern L. Cunningham and Joseph Hentges
1992	*The Study of the American School Superintendency*	Thomas Glass
2000	*The Study of the American School Superintendency*	Thomas Glass, Lars Björk, and C. Cryss Brunner
2010	*The American School Superintendent: 2010 Decennial Study*	Theodore Kowalski, Robert McCord, George Petersen, I. Phillip Young, and Noelle Ellerson
2020	*The American School Superintendent: 2020 Decennial Study*	Christopher H. Tienken, Editor

tions elicited quantitative and qualitative responses from participants. The majority of the questions were based on the 2010 study, allowing for longitudinal analyses of superintendent perceptions, while some questions were unique to this study. For example, questions about social media use, issues around equity and race, and the use of executive coaching were unique to the 2020 version of the survey.

POPULATION

The identified population for the study included all superintendents employed by local school districts. The population for study was approximately thirteen thousand active superintendents. The population excluded state superintendents and superintendents of state or regional education service centers.

DATA COLLECTION

Multiple email communications were sent to national education organizations and notices were posted on the AASA website to inform the superintendents about the study and to request their participation. The study principal investigator also conducted information sessions and sent informative emails to some of the heads of state and county associations in order to raise awareness of the survey.

The digital survey was emailed to all members of AASA and all active superintendents, approximately thirteen thousand administrators. The survey was live for about six weeks. Secondary data were collected via document analyses of previous decennial studies and mid-decade salary studies (e.g., 2000, 2010, and 2015) and empirical studies of the superintendent conducted since 2000.

AASA officials sent emails to all members that included an overview of the survey and directions on how to access and complete the survey. AASA opened the survey on April 21,

2019, via an Internet link. The survey officially closed on June 1, 2019. AASA officials sent out reminder emails to participants approximately once a week while the survey was live.

SAMPLE

The final sample included 1,218 respondents (n=1,218) from 45 states (see table 2.2). Superintendents from Illinois and Minnesota constituted the largest percentage of responses in the sample, 11% and 6.45% respectively; and 1,100 of the 1,218 participants responded to the question that identified the state in which they worked.

The majority of the respondents worked in rural districts, 54.78%, and suburban districts, 20.76% (see table 2.3). Approximately 73% of the respondents were male and 27% were female, representing an increase in female superintendents compared to the 2010 respondents in which 76% of respondents were male and 24% were female. Approximately 62% of the respondents worked in districts with 1,000 or more students enrolled, with 33% working in districts with 1,000–2,999 students enrolled (see table 2.4).

INSTRUMENTATION

The survey had seventy-six questions and included five parts: (1) district and personal demographics, (2) career pathways, (3) professional learning, (4) current work, and (5) community relations. There were 11 questions related to demographics, 14 questions related to career pathways, 11 questions aimed at professional learning, 24 questions related to current work, and 15 questions for community relations. The final question on the survey asked superintendents if they were willing to participate in a follow-up phone interview.

AASA conducted member checks of each survey question with a panel of experts. The panel of experts included AASA members, AASA organizational officials, and study staff. Then the survey was piloted with a group of practicing superintendents to ensure appropriate functioning of the online survey mechanism, clarity of questions, and ease of use for the participants. Participants were asked to complete the proposed survey and to make recommendations about the content of the questions, the formatting, and the overall presentation. Changes to language, content, and format were made and the panel of experts reviewed all changes prior to the administration of the survey.

Some questions on the survey were dichotomous in nature and required only one response, whereas other questions allowed for multiple responses. There was no mechanism for respondents to mark a question as *Not applicable* or *No response*.

Table 2.2. State-by-State Response Counts and Percentages to Q1: In Which State Is Your School District Located?

Responses	Count	%
AL	13	1.18%
AK	17	1.55%
AZ	14	1.27%
AR	60	5.45%
CA	27	2.45%
CO	41	3.73%
CT	9	0.82%
DE	0	0.00%

DC	0	0.00%
FL	1	0.09%
GA	5	0.45%
HI	0	0.00%
ID	11	1.00%
IL	121	11.00%
IN	63	5.73%
IA	29	2.64%
KS	16	1.45%
KY	0	0.00%
LA	2	0.18%
ME	7	0.64%
MD	4	0.36%
MA	11	1.00%
MI	29	2.64%
MN	71	6.45%
MS	5	0.45%
MO	24	2.18%
MT	42	3.82%
NE	10	0.91%
NV	2	0.18%
NH	20	1.82%
NJ	18	1.64%
NM	3	0.27%
NY	48	4.36%
NC	15	1.36%
ND	4	0.36%
OH	27	2.45%
OK	65	5.91%
OR	37	3.36%
PA	30	2.73%
RI	3	0.27%
SC	0	0.00%
SD	2	0.18%
TN	12	1.09%
TX	42	3.82%
UT	4	0.36%
VT	13	1.18%
VA	27	2.45%
WA	17	1.55%
WV	2	0.18%

WI	58	5.27%
WY	17	1.55%
Other	2	0.18%
Total	**1,100**	

Table 2.3. Geographic Location of the Respondents' Districts to Q2: Which One of the Following Best Describes the Geographic Location of Your School District?

Responses	Count	%
Urban	68	5.60%
Suburban	252	20.76%
Small town/city	229	18.86%
Rural	665	54.78%
Total	**1,214**	

Table 2.4. District Enrollment of Respondents to Q3: How Many Students Were Enrolled in Your District as of October 1, 2018?

Responses	Count	%
Fewer than 300	143	11.76%
300 to 999	326	26.81%
1,000 to 2,999	400	32.89%
3,000 to 4,999	113	9.29%
5,000 to 9,999	118	9.70%
10,000 to 24,999	83	6.83%
25,000 to 49,999	23	1.89%
50,000 to 99,999	6	0.49%
100,000 or more	4	0.33%
Total Responses	**1,216**	

DATA ANALYSIS

An AASA data analyst downloaded responses from completed surveys to the *K12 Insight* platform. The responses represent a working sample of the total population of employed superintendents. Over 660,000 cells of data were collected from 1,218 participants. Participation varied by state with some states accounting for a greater percentage of the responses than others. This is due in part because some states have countywide districts with one superintendent per county, whereas other states have a superintendent for every town. For example, Maryland runs county school districts and has twenty-four superintendents whereas West Virginia has approximately forty-six superintendents spread throughout the local towns.

Tables were produced for the aggregate results from each survey question. Aggregate tables included counts and percentages. Then crosstabs were created for various questions. Almost nine hundred two-level and three-level crosstabs were run with the seventy-six questions. A random sample of crosstabs were reviewed by a team of three researchers to check for accuracy.

MISSING DATA

There was no mechanism for respondents to submit a response such as *Not applicable* or *No response*. This caused some instances of missing data. A review of each aggregate table and approximately three hundred crosstab tables indicated that the missing data rarely reached 2% of the total sample for questions with missing data.

The majority of missing data appeared to be *Missing at Random* (MAR) in the aggregate tables. However, a common feature of missing data that accounted for more than 2% of the responses in a question seemed to be with questions in which the most likely response would have been *Not applicable*. Four questions from the seventy-six-question survey had missing data that exceeded 5% of the sample: Questions 1, 55, 67, 68, and 72. Three questions had missing responses from 3% of the sample: Questions 40, 61, and 63.

Approximately 17% of the participants did not respond to Question 55: *Who led the conversations related to issues of equity?* The most likely explanation for the high percentage of missing data is that the question was not applicable to all respondents. Only respondents who have had specific discussions of equity in their district would be able to answer the question.

Approximately 8% (7.7) of the sample did not respond to Question 67: *Which of the following issues has generated political action among groups in your district in the past three years?* This question would only be applicable to respondents who had issues that generated political action in the last three years.

Questions 68 and 72 focused on social media use. Almost 10% of the sample did not answer Question 68: *Do you maintain any of the following social media accounts and use them to promote the work of the school district?* Again, superintendents who did not use social media or did not use them to promote the work of the school district would not answer this question. Almost 6% of the sample did not answer Question 72: *Rate your level of activity on social media.* This question was not applicable to those superintendents who do not use social media.

SUMMARY

The difficulty in examining the complexity of the superintendency and those who occupy the position cannot be overstated. AASA endeavored to collect data on the various intricacies of the position, but a single survey cannot capture all the meaningful aspects of the position. The results, while wide-ranging and generally representative of the population, should be interpreted with care. The study relied on a non-randomized design and voluntary return by participants. The sampling could have been complicated by the reliance on a third-party vendor to accurately identify and contact the population of potential respondents. Another potential limitation was the use of the term "minority" in some of the questions. The intent of the survey designers was to use the term to describe the non-Caucasian groups within the national population. That was not clearly stated to participants. Similarly, the term "of color" as used in phrases such as *Superintendents of Color* refers to respondents who identified their race/ethnicity as something other than *Caucasian.*

Sweeping decisions or conclusions should not be made from the results of this report alone. Readers should interpret the findings in the context of previous studies and recent literature.

Chapter 3 provides results about the demographic characteristics of who becomes a superintendent. Interpretations are provided within the context of the broader literature.

Chapter Three

Superintendents and the Intersections of Race, Gender, and District Composition

Margaret Grogan and Angel Miles Nash

This chapter presents a portrait of the 2020 demographic characteristics of superintendents and the districts in which they work. We provide an analysis of the nexus between superintendents' identity and district demographic factors including district size, district location, and student population characteristics. We compare select findings of the 2020 survey to those from the 2010 survey and other relevant literature. We conclude the chapter with takeaways for current and aspiring superintendents.

WHO IS CURRENTLY SUPERINTENDENT OF SCHOOLS IN THE UNITED STATES?

We are pleased to report the data disaggregated by gender and by race/ethnicity for the first time in the history of the AASA decennial studies. The data from the 2020 AASA Decennial Study of the Superintendent suggest there have been small gains in the demographic diversity of the U.S. superintendent since 2010, but the profession has made substantial gains in terms of gender equity since 2000.

The 2020 AASA Decennial Study reported a gender breakdown of 26.7% females and 72.9% males compared to 24.1% females and 75.9% males in 2010; this marks an increase of more than 2.5% in the proportion of women leading in the role (see figure 3.1). Although a 2.5% difference in a decade appears small, the percentage of female superintendents in 2020 (26.7%) is more than double the percentage documented in 2000 (13.1%) as reported by Kowalski, McCord, Peterson, Young, and Ellerson (2011).

There have also been small, yet consistent gains in the racial/ethnic diversity of superintendents. Preliminary figures in each category indicate similar numbers of men and women who do not identify as white: of the Native American and Native Alaskans, there were 14 (1.1%) men and 7 (0.6%) women, of the Asian Americans, there was 1 man (0.08 %) and 1 woman (0.08%), of the black and African American respondents there were 23 (1.8%) men and 18 women (1.4%), of the Hawaiian and Pacific Islanders there was 1 man (0.08%) and 1 woman (0.08%), of the Latinx there were 17 men (1.3%) and 13 women (1.0%), and there were 5 men (0.4%) and 3 (0.2%) women who identified as other.

Approximately 8.2% of respondents identified as superintendents of color in 2020, compared to 6% in 2010, and only 5% in 2000 (Kowalski et al., 2011, pp. 19–20). The term "of color" used in phrases such as *Superintendents of Color* refers to respondents who identified their race/ethnicity as something other than *Caucasian.* Further, of the superintendents of color, nearly 42% are women. Women of color comprise 12.9% of all female superintendents and men of color account for nearly 7% of all male superintendents. We are pleased to report small but steady increases in the number of superintendents of color nationwide, and particularly women of color, which nearly doubled the 6.8% of the sample reported in a 2007 national study (Brunner and Grogan, 2007).

Although demographic diversity in the position of superintendent appears to be changing slowly, the position of superintendent is much more diverse than its counterpart in the business world, the chief executive officer (CEO). The percentage of women and leaders of color in the top leadership position in education is well above the 5.4% of S&P 500 companies led by a woman and the 5% of the Russell 3000 companies that have a woman in the top position. There were only four black CEOs leading Fortune 500 companies in 2019 (Akhtar, 2019). Nevertheless, while the trends are headed in the right direction in education, the low proportion of women and individuals of color in the most powerful district position in education is still troubling.

Recent trends in the student population underscore a demographic imbalance between school and district leadership and the students they serve. In 2017, only 51% of the school-age children in the United States identified as white (NCES, 2019). Even the teaching population, which has been slow to diversify across all states, is beginning to look different nationwide with 20% of teachers of color in 2016 (NCES, 2018). Public school principals of color reached 22% in the 2017–2018 school year (NCES, 2019).

Gender equity in the principalship is also increasing. Women now account for 67% of elementary principals, 40% of middle school principals, and 33% of high school principals (NCES, 2019). Just as the demographics of school principals changed over time, we predict the demographic characteristics of superintendents will change in the decades to come based on the changes in the teaching population and continuing demographic evolution taking place in the principal ranks.

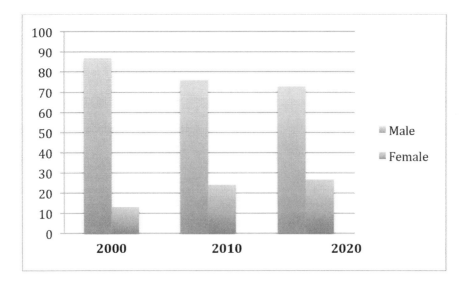

Figure 3.1.   Gender Trends of the American Superintendent, 2000–2020.

SCHOOLS AND STUDENTS SERVED BY SUPERINTENDENTS

The makeup of a school district influences the responsibilities of the superintendent in varying ways. Therefore, it is important to understand districts' overall characteristics including their size, location, socioeconomic standings, as well as the backgrounds of students and communities such as their race/ethnicity and linguistics. A deeper look at the race/ethnicity and gender of superintendents also offers insight into the positionality of the leaders who are charged with considering what is best for students across the country.

THE MAKEUP OF DISTRICTS

About 3% of the respondents in this study were employed in very large districts in 2019. Almost 12% (11.76%) were employed in districts with enrollments of 300 or less; an increase from 9% in the same size district in 2010. The distribution of respondents by district enrollment in the 2020 study was similar to the distribution in the 2010 study with a slight increase in respondents from districts under 3,000 students (71.46% compared to 68.3% in 2010).

The results reveal that more women serve in districts of all sizes. Although most women superintendents still serve in districts with enrollments of 3,000 students or fewer (71% of all women), there is more female representation across all district enrollment categories. Data from the 2010 Decennial Study (Kowalski et al., 2011, pp. 86–87) showed a disproportionate number of women (59.3%) led districts with student enrollments between 300 and 2,999.

As of 2020, except for districts under 300 students, where women make up 31.47% of the total population of superintendents, female superintendents account for about 25% of districts between 300 and 2,999 students, and about 29% of districts with enrollments between 5,000 and 24,999. Women moved into superintendencies in larger districts between 2010 and 2020. An interesting note is that though the raw numbers are very small, women are superintendents in some of the largest districts in the country; they lead 33% in districts with enrollments between 50,000 and 99,999 and 75% of the districts with student enrollments of more than 100,000. Superintendents of color are also serving in districts of all sizes. However, it is somewhat surprising to note that 40% of the women of color superintendents served in districts of over 5,000 compared to just over 30% of the men of color superintendents.

Districts are more diverse than ever before. One of the sub questions on the survey asked superintendents about the percent of racial/ethnic minorities in their district. As noted in chapter 2, there was no definition of the term "minority" provided to the respondents. We find this very troubling, especially in terms of what constitutes a minority of students in a district. In past surveys, the term racial/ethnic minority was meant to connote non-white populations, and although not defined for the 2020 survey, the intended definition was the same as in 2010. Clearly, the last category on the 5-point scale of the survey, *51 percent or more*, refers to a majority of the students in the district.

Overall, the 2020 survey shows an increase in the percentage of racial/ethnic minority students being served. Compared to the 2010 study, there was a slight increase in districts serving *51% or more* students who were non-white: 15.44%, up almost 1% from 14.5%. The largest change was in the first category, *5% or under*, which dropped from 47% in 2010 to 34% in 2020. Currently almost 52% of districts serve between 6% to 50% racial/ethnic minority students compared to only 39% of districts in the 2010 study. The change underscores the demographic evolution of the United States and the predictions that more than 50% of the population will be non-white or "minority white" by 2045 (Frey, 2018).

There are more superintendents of color in districts with larger populations of racial/ethnic minority students. Almost 78% of superintendents of color serve in districts with more than 26% racial/ethnic minority students. Of districts serving *51% or more* racial/ethnic minority students, nearly a third are led by superintendents of color and 32% are led by women, of which 37% are women of color. Districts with more than 26% racial/ethnic minority students appear to attract proportionally more women and more superintendents of color than other districts.

CONFRONTING ISSUES OF RACE

Two questions on this survey extended our understanding of how superintendents view the importance of leading conversations about race and how prepared they felt to do so. One question asked how important it is to lead conversations about race in the district and community. Another asked how prepared the superintendent felt to lead such conversations.

Although this subject is addressed in more detail in chapter 6, we provide a summary of some results in light of the demographic trends of superintendents and students. Eleven percent of white superintendents indicated it was *Not important* to lead conversations about race in the district and community. Of the 89% of white superintendents who said that it was *Important* or *Extremely important*, only 42% of white men said it was extremely important compared to 47% of white women, whereas 63% of women of color superintendents said it was *Extremely important* compared to 52% of men of color.

Although 80% of all superintendents said they were *Very well* or *Sufficiently prepared* to lead conversations about race, only 21% of all superintendents said they were *Very well prepared*. However, 43% of all superintendents of color felt *Very well prepared* to lead conversations about race/ethnicity. Although the survey does not inquire into how successful superintendents are in engaging their communities around issues of race, gaps emerge between the level of preparedness to do the work and the belief that it is important to do so. These data suggest that superintendents of color are twice as likely as white superintendents to actually lead a conversation in their district. Perhaps the likelihood of a superintendent leading a discussion about race depends on the demographic diversity of the district.

When we examine districts by percentage of ethnic/minority students and how prepared the superintendent felt to lead such conversations, we find that over half of the superintendents who described themselves as *Very well prepared* served in districts with 15% or fewer racial/ethnic minority students. However, of the superintendents serving districts with 51% or more non-white students, 94% were *Very well* or *Sufficiently prepared* to lead a conversation compared to the 75% of superintendents in districts with 5% or fewer racial/ethnic minority students, who felt at least *Sufficiently prepared.* The data suggest that as district diversity increased, a larger percentage of the superintendents felt prepared to lead conversations about race.

Of the superintendents of color, 50% of superintendents who identified as black or African American reported they were *Very well prepared* to lead conversations about race whereas 40% of superintendents who identified as Hispanic/Latinx reported being *Very well prepared.* Only about 20% of white superintendents reported being *Very well prepared* to lead conversations about race and an equal percentage noted being *Not at all prepared* to lead such conversations, the highest percentage of *Not at all prepared* of any racial group.

LEADING SCHOOLS IN DIFFERENT CONTEXTS

The disaggregated data available from this study illumined the findings related to who leads schools by the type of locations in which they are situated (i.e., urban, suburban, small town/ city, or rural). The breakdown of school types across the country are as follows: 5.60% urban, 20.76% suburban, 18.86% small town/city, and 54.78% rural. Across these school types there was telling information regarding the backgrounds of superintendents who lead the districts.

Most urban school districts are led by white men (40%) followed by those led by white women (22.86%). Black or African American men lead 12.86% of urban school districts, and black or African American women lead 8.57% of urban school districts. The urban districts led by Hispanic/Latinx men (7.14%) and women (4.29%) represent positive increases from previous years.

In suburban school districts, slightly different proportions emerged. Although the majority of suburban school districts are led by white men (68.55%), and white women (23.79%), each of the remaining demographics are 2% or less. The third highest are black or African American women and Hispanic/Latinx men, which both tied at 2.02%.

The leadership in small towns and city districts reflect statistics that are very similar to those in suburban schools. However, Native American or Native Alaskan men are superintendents of 1.77% of school districts, which represents the largest ratio of school districts led by this demographic. The remaining ratios, less than 2% of remaining schools, are led by superintendents who are Native American, black or African American, or Hispanic.

Finally, because a majority of the respondents worked in rural locations, it is important to note who leads in these areas. The percentages of those who lead the most often increase in the category, and in doing so, further align with the overall percentages reported in the 2020 Decennial Survey. By way of example, 70.02% of rural districts are led by white men, and 22.37% are led by white women. In comparison, 1.67% and 0.76% of rural school districts are led by black or African American men and black or African American women respectively. Native American or Native Alaskan men lead 1.22% of schools and Native American or Native Alaskan women lead 0.91% of districts. Evenly, Hispanic/Latinx women and men lead 0.76% of rural schools.

ENGLISH LANGUAGE LEARNERS

Superintendents are tasked with offering programming that supports English language learners. As the emergent bilingual population continues to grow in the United States, the population of students who speak languages other than English at home, superintendents must find ways to meet their unique needs. The linguistics abilities and learning needs of emergent bilinguals call for leaders to provide an education that includes and responds to diverse cultures and familial backgrounds. Of the school districts with 26% to 50% students who are emergent bilinguals, 80.65% are led by white superintendents and 19.35% are led by superintendents of color. Most of the leaders of color are black or African American (12.91%).

It was more common for school districts with 51% or more students who were emergent bilingual to be led by Hispanic/Latinx superintendents (33.33%). The majority of school districts educate populations with less than 5% of students who are emergent bilingual, with 768 respondents falling into this category. It is important to note that among the distinctions, the majority of the Native American or Native Alaskan superintendents serve districts in this category, at 1.95%, which is the highest percentage led by this demographic (see table 3.1).

FREE AND REDUCED LUNCH

The socioeconomic influences on education are important factors to consider for district leaders. Financial abundance and strain affect students' lives in varying ways and those strains require school leaders to customize solutions at the local level. The majority of respondents were superintendents of schools that served populations in which 51% or more students were eligible for free/reduced lunch. Of the 484 school districts in that category, 15.08% were led by superintendents of color (see table 3.2).

DEMOGRAPHICS

Prior research on the superintendency revealed that men and women experience the work of leadership differently on a personal level. For instance, in 2010 more male superintendents were married compared to females (93.6% and 81.8% respectively, p. 89). In 2010 fewer male superintendents than women were divorced (3.7% compared to 8.8% p. 89). Results from the 2020 survey demonstrated that 86% of all superintendents reported being married or partnered (89% of male superintendents and 82% of female superintendents) and 4.2% of men and 8.3% of women were divorced. However, when the figures are disaggregated according to gender and race and ethnicity, only 65% of women of color superintendents were married or part-nered compared to 85% of men of color superintendents and both men and women of color were twice as likely as white men and women to be divorced.

When asked about changes to their personal lives they or their spouse/partner made to accommodate the demands of the superintendent's job, 46% of all respondents reported mov-ing to a new location. When disaggregated by race/ethnicity, only 30% of the women of color superintendents reported moving. Slightly less than a third of superintendents (31.2%) re-ported that their spouse/partner changed jobs to support the demands of the superintendency. The largest proportion of superintendents reporting this change were 35% of male superinten-dents of color compared to 27% of white women who comprised the smallest proportion. In other words, fewer superintendents who identified as white women reported having a spouse who changed jobs to accommodate their superintendency compared to any other demographic group.

It is encouraging to find that only 3.4% of women superintendents report a delay in having children and only 8.3% of women superintendents report having fewer or no children because of the demands of the job. However, the 2015 AASA mid-decade survey found that 37.3% of women superintendents were childless (Robinson, Shakeshaft, Grogan, and Sherman New-comb, 2017).

Superintendents are moving into the position at earlier ages than previously reported. According to the 2020 survey, the majority of respondents (59%) were superintendent by the time they were forty-five compared to only 49.5% of superintendents in the 2010 survey who were superintendent by that age. Particularly surprising are the number of young superinten-dents of color; 58% of the men of color superintendents and 48% of the women of color superintendents were superintendents by the time they were forty-five. And in contrast to earlier studies, 41% of women superintendents were superintendents by that age, including 38% of white women superintendents. In stark contrast, only 10.28% of women superinten-dents were forty-five or under in 2010.

Gender differences have also been found in examining the reasons superintendents be-lieved the school board hired them. The importance of this question for women aspiring to the superintendency is that for many years key qualifications for the position such as the ability to

Table 3.1.   Gender and Racial/Ethnicity Breakdown of Superintendents and the Percentage of ELL Students in School Districts

	Native American or Native Alaskan	Asian	Black or African American	Native Hawaiian or Other Pacific Islander	Hispanic/Latinx	White	Other	Total
Less than/equal to 5%								
Male	1.30%	0.13%	1.17%	0.13%	0.39%	71.88%	0.52%	75.52%
Female	0.65%	0.13%	0.91%	0.13%	0.39%	21.88%	0%	24.09%
Total	1.95%	0.26%	2.08%	0.26%	0.78%	94.14%	0.52%	100%
6 to 15%								
Male	1.17%	0%	2.33%	0%	1.95%	65.76%	0%	71.21%
Female	0%	0%	2.33%	0%	1.95%	23.35%	0.39%	28.02%
Total	1.17%	0%	4.67%	0%	3.89%	89.88%	0.39%	100%
16 to 25%								
Male	0%	0%	1.90%	0%	5.71%	58.10%	0%	65.71%
Female	0.95%	0%	2.86%	0%	2.86%	25.71%	1.90%	34.29%
Total	0.95%	0%	4.76%	0%	8.57%	83.81%	1.90%	100%
26 to 50%								
Male	0%	0%	9.68%	0%	1.61%	50.00%	1.61%	62.90%
Female	1.61%	0%	3.23%	0%	1.61%	30.65%	0%	37.10%
Total	1.61%	0%	12.90%	0%	3.23%	80.65%	1.61%	100%
51% or More								
Male	0%	0%	0%	0%	22.22%	55.56%	0%	77.78%
Female	0%	0%	0%	0%	11.11%	11.11%	0%	22.22%
Total	0%	0%	0%	0%	33.33%	66.67%	0%	100%

Table 3.2. Gender and Racial/Ethnicity Breakdown of Superintendents and the Percentage of Students Eligible for Free or Reduced-Price Lunches in Their School Districts

	Native American or Native Alaskan	Asian	Black or African American	Native Hawaiian or Other Pacific Islander	Hispanic/Latinx	White	Other	Total
Less Than/Equal to 5%								
Male	0%	0%	4.35%	0%	0%	65.22%	0%	69.57%
Female	0%	0%	0%	0%	0%	26.09%	0%	26.09%
Total	0%	0%	4.35%	0%	0%	95.65%	0%	100%
6 to 15%								
Male	0%	0%	1.35%	0%	0%	78.38%	0%	79.73%
Female	0%	0%	0%	0%	0%	20.27%	0%	20.27%
Total	0%	0%	1.35%	0%	0%	98.65%	0%	100%
16 to 25%								
Male	0%	0.71%	0%	0%	0%	70.71%	0%	71.43%
Female	0.71%	0.71%	0.71%	0%	0.71%	25.00%	0.71%	28.57%
Total	0.71%	1.43%	0.71%	0%	0.71%	95.71%	0.71%	100%
26 to 50%								
Male	0.42%	0%	0.84%	0%	0.84%	71.76%	0.21%	74.06%
Female	0.42%	0%	0.63%	0.21%	0.84%	23.64%	0%	25.73%
Total	0.84%	0%	1.46%	0.21%	1.67%	95.61%	0.21%	100%
51% or More								
Male	2.27%	0%	3.51%	0.21%	2.48%	61.98%	0.83%	71.28%
Female	0.83%	0%	2.89%	0%	1.65%	22.31%	0.41%	28.10%
Total	3.10%	0%	6.40%	0.21%	4.13%	84.92%	1.24%	100%

manage fiscal resources and to lead renovation and/or construction projects were firmly embedded in the male trajectory toward the position (Grogan, 1996). However, since the No
Child Left Behind (NCLB) Act of 2001, much more attention has been focused on instruction
and the ability to be a change agent.

For example, almost 58% of all superintendents reported that the school board hired them
to be an instructional leader in 2020, compared to a mere 20% of all superintendents in 2010.
Seventy-two percent of the women in this survey believed this to be one of the three primary
reasons for their hire compared to only 33% of women in 2010. Only about 52% of male
superintendents believed they were hired to be instructional leaders. In addition, a larger
proportion of superintendents believed they were hired to be change agents in 2020 than in
2010 (46% compared to 25%). By far the largest proportion of superintendents to give this
reason in 2020 were women of color superintendents, 65% of whom believed this was one of
the primary reasons they were hired.

CONCLUSION

Although there is only slow progress to report in terms of the overall percentage of women
superintendents in 2019 (26.68% compared to 24.1% in 2010), as noted in the first section of
the chapter, the percentage of women in the top leadership position in education is well above
the 5.4% of S&P 500 companies led by a woman and only 5% of the Russell 3000 companies
that have a woman in the top position. Slow progress is being made by superintendents of
color, but women of color superintendents have made significant gains, moving from 6.7% of
women superintendents in 2007 to 13.3% in 2020. Both are promising trends.

The rapidly changing demographics of school districts, as reported in this survey, might be
why superintendents are expected to be change agents more than before. On the one hand, as
districts become more diverse, more opportunities might be provided for superintendents who
can effectively address social justice issues. However, the finding that 65% of women of color
believe they were hired as change agents continues to be a double-edged sword. Brunner and
Grogan (2007) found that women of color were disproportionately hired in extremely volatile
districts putting them greatly at risk of remaining in the position. Thus, more research is
needed to understand the extent to which leading such districts is desirable.

Overall, the major takeaways from this chapter for women and women and men of color
aspiring to the superintendency in 2020 are that there are fewer gender differences in choice of
district, although very few individuals of color are serving in rural districts. There are few
differences in the age aspirants become superintendent regardless of gender or race/ethnicity.
The playing field is slowly becoming more level than 2010 in many respects. For women it is
still an advantage to offer strong instructional expertise under the Every Student Succeeds Act
(ESSA) 2015, as it has been since the passage of NCLB 2001 (Brunner and Grogan, 2007;
Grogan and Shakeshaft, 2011). Hispanic/Latinx aspirants clearly have an advantage in gaining
a superintendency in districts with large populations of bilingual and emerging bilingual
students.

Because leadership preparation for women and men begins as teachers, the continued
upward trajectories for women and for women and men of color are very important. Students
need to see role models not only to shape their own aspirations of leadership but also to learn
more effectively. As research indicates, the lived experiences of leaders best prepare them to
detect and address marginalizing conditions under which students struggle to achieve (Grogan
and Shakeshaft, 2011). It is most likely the lived experiences of superintendents of color that

have prepared them to engage their communities around issues of race and ethnicity, a highly valued skill as districts across the country become more polarized and more diverse.

REFERENCES

Akhtar, A. (2019, Nov. 1). "Corporate America Is Seeing a Spike in the Age of CEOs Being Hired and Yes, They're Overwhelmingly White Men." *Business Insider*. Retrieved from https://www.businessinsider.com/corporate-america-ceos-are-getting-older-mostly-white-2019-10.

Brunner, C. C., and Grogan, M. (2007). *Women Leading School Systems: Uncommon Roads to Fulfillment*. Lanham, MD: Rowman & Littlefield Education.

Every Student Succeeds Act (Pub. L. 114–95) 2015.

Frey, W. H. (2018, Mar. 14). "The US Will Become Minority White in 2045 Census Predicts." *Brookings*. Retrieved from https://www.brookings.edu/blog/the-avenue/2018/03/14/the-us-will-become-minority-white-in-2045-census-projects/.

Grogan, M. (1996). *Voices of Women Aspiring to the Superintendency*. Albany, NY: SUNY Press.

Grogan, M., and Shakeshaft, C. (2011). *Women and Educational Leadership*. San Francisco, CA: Jossey-Bass.

Kowalski, T. J., McCord, R. S., Peterson, G. J., Young, P. I., and Ellerson, N. M. (2011). *The American School Superintendent: 2010 Decennial Study*. Lanham, MD: Rowman & Littlefield.

National Center for Education Statistics (2018). *The Condition of Education 2018* (Report No. NCES 2018–144). Washington, DC: United States Department of Education.

National Center for Education Statistics (2019). *The Condition of Education 2019* (Report No. NCES 2018–144). Washington, DC: United States Department of Education.

No Child Left Behind Act of 2001, 20 U.S.C. § 6319 (2001).

Robinson, K., Shakeshaft, C., Grogan, M., and Newcomb, W. S. (2017). *Necessary but Not Sufficient: The Continuing Inequality between Men and Women in Educational Leadership, Findings from the American Association of School Administrators Mid-Decade Survey*. In *Frontiers in Education* 2 (12), (1–12). doi:10.3389/feduc.2017.00012.

Chapter Four

Career Pathways of Superintendents

George J. Petersen and David G. Title

Public education has seen marked changes in the ten years since the 2010 AASA Decennial Study was published. The intervening ten years have been perhaps one of the most consequential eras in education history. Although the changes did not specifically target superintendents, we hypothesize the work life and career patterns of a superintendent may have changed as a result. As described in chapter 3, these changes in the educational landscape seem to be influencing the age at which an educational leader becomes a superintendent of schools, why they are chosen for the role, and how long they plan to serve in it.

PURPOSE

The purpose of this chapter is to present the results on the career pathways of superintendents. Content is divided into three sections. The first section examines and expands data presented in chapter 3 related to accessing a first superintendency. The second section examines data about professional experiences while serving as a superintendent, and the third section includes opinion data about future roles and plans after leaving the superintendency.

PROFESSIONAL EXPERIENCES

We conducted an analysis of the professional experiences of superintendents using the results of a survey question that asked participants to identify all the positions that they had at least one year of full-time experience. Ninety-six percent of superintendents reported that they had experience as a classroom teacher for at least one year and over four-fifths (80%) had served as a school principal (see table 4.1). The data also revealed that over three-quarters of respondents (80%) had served in some district level leadership capacity as a director, coordinator, assistant, or associate superintendent. Findings reveal that superintendents' experience in serving as an assistant principal parallel the results from the 2010 study (Kowalski et al., 2010) in which approximately 53% of participants also served at least one year as an assistant principal.

TEACHING TENURE

Results from previous studies consistently demonstrate that the career path for most superintendents begins as a classroom teacher and then building-level leadership (Kowalski et al., 2010). As reported in the 2010 study, several states waived certification and experience prerequisites to superintendent licensing, yet data reveal that most of the superintendents participating in this study have followed what earlier studies have shown to be a more traditional career progression into the superintendency (Glass et al., 2000). The career trajectory for most begins in the classroom and progresses through the assistant principalship and/or the principalship.

More than half (62%) of superintendents had between 5–12 years of classroom teaching experience and for almost all of the respondents (97%), their classroom experience was in a public school setting (see table 4.2).

Table 4.1. Professional Experiences

Responses	Count	%
Classroom teacher	1,173	96%
Assistant principal	647	53%
Principal	1,030	84%
Master teacher or instructional coach	115	9%
School counselor	50	4%
District-level director/coordinator/supervisor	555	45%
Assistant/associate/deputy superintendent	434	35%
College or university professor or administrator	187	15%
Military	52	4%
Non-education related executive position	81	7%
Other	63	5%
Total Responses	4,387	

Note: Multiple answers per participant possible. Percentages added may exceed 100 since a participant may select more than one answer for this question.

Table 4.2. Teaching Tenure

Responses (Years)	Count	%
0–1	23	1.9%
2–4	183	15.2%
5–8	458	38.1%
9–12	292	24.3%
13 or more	247	20.5%
Total Responses	1,203	100%

AGE OF FIRST SUPERINTENDENCY

The 2010 study (Kowalski et al.) revealed that the modal age for first-time superintendents was 46- to 50-years-old; approximately one-fourth of the superintendents entered the position in this age range in that study.

Collectively, data in table 4.3 reveal that the first assignment as a superintendent continues to be during mid-career stages (i.e., chronological ages between 41 and 55 years). Sixty percent of respondents were between the ages of 41–55 when they accepted their first superintendency. Similar to the 2010 study (13.3%), 13.1% of respondents were less than 36 years of age when they became superintendents.

Table 4.3. Age of First Superintendency

Responses	Count	%
Less than 36	159	13.1%
36–40	227	18.7%
41–45	306	25.2%
46–50	249	20.5%
51–55	177	14.6%
56–60	75	6.2%
61–65	13	1.1%
66+	3	0.3%
Decline to answer	4	0.3%
Total responses	1,213	100%

COLLEGE DEGREES EARNED

Although not required for state licensing, the number of superintendents with doctorates remained virtually unchanged since 2000. In this study nearly 44% superintendents received a terminal degree (i.e., PhD or EdD). These findings are similar to the 2010 (Kowalski et al.) and the 2000 (Glass et al.) studies; both found 45.3% held a doctoral degree (see table 4.4). Table 4.5 reveals that a majority of terminal degrees for participating superintendents were in the areas of Educational Leadership (53%) and Educational Administration and Supervision (34%). This is not surprising provided that a terminal degree in leadership or administration would be traditional areas of study for those aspiring to school leadership and administration positions.

INSTRUMENTAL INDIVIDUALS

Superintendents in this study were asked to identify the individuals who were most instrumental in assisting them in becoming superintendents. This question is new for the 2020 study. The data suggest that almost all superintendents began as teachers and then transitioned into building leadership positions. At some point the respondents determined that the next step in their career was to seek the leadership role of superintendent.

Reasons varied, but previous research suggests that rarely do education leaders make the decision to become a superintendent in a vacuum. In this study, respondents were asked to

Table 4.4.　College Degrees Earned

Responses	Count	%
Bachelor's	1,051	86.5%
Master's	1,137	93.6%
Ph.D.	109	9.0%
Ed.D.	429	35.3%
J.D.	6	0.5%
MBA	16	1.3%
Educational specialist	379	31.2%
Other	79	6.5%
Total unique responses	1,215	
Total responses	3,206	

Note: Multiple answers per participant possible. Percentages added may exceed 100
since a participant may select more than one answer for this question.

Table 4.5.　Field of Study of Highest Degree Earned

Responses	Count	%
Education (general)	64	5.2%
Early childhood/elementary/middle/secondary teaching	7	0.6%
Special education	13	1.0%
Curriculum and instruction	28	2.3%
Education leadership	640	53.0%
Education administration/Supervision	415	34.0%
Finance/Business	10	0.8%
Legal	4	0.3%
Other (please specify)	34	2.8%
Total Responses	1,215	100%

identify individuals who were instrumental in helping them become superintendents. Table 4.6 reveals that the most instrumental individuals in the careers of these superintendents were their superintendent supervisors (65.3%), spouses or relatives (52.3%) and colleagues (48.5%). These findings are consistent with research that has shown that along with superintendent preparation programs, many individuals who aspire to the superintendency seek the advice and mentorship of a sitting superintendent (Callan and Levinson, 2011).

PUBLIC SCHOOL DISTRICTS SERVED

In the past, research has demonstrated that prior experience as a superintendent has been a highly valued criterion for many school boards seeking to employ a new superintendent (Heneman, Judge, and Kammeyer-Muller, 2018). Comparing the findings in the 2010 study and this study, the number of public school districts in

Table 4.6. Individuals Instrumental in Helping You Become a Superintendent

Responses	Count	%
Spouse or relative	622	52.3%
Friend	322	27.1%
Professor	256	21.5%
Colleague	577	48.5%
Supervisor (principal)	180	15.1%
Supervisor (superintendent)	776	65.3%
Mentor (non-supervisory)	374	31.5%
Other (please specify)	74	6.2%
Total Unique Responses	1,189	
Total Responses	3,181	

Note: Multiple answers per participant possible. Percentages added may exceed 100 since a participant may select more than one answer for this question.

which a superintendent served has remained virtually unchanged. In 2010, 59.3% of superintendents had only held the position in one school district and 22.9% had served as superintendent in more than two districts (Kowalski et al., 2010).

In this study, the former figure increased slightly, and the latter remained the same. The data suggest that over three-quarters (84.2%) of current superintendents are in their first or second district. This implies that superintendents are not moving rapidly from district to district, and that is a trend that has been consistent since 2010 (see table 4.7).

Table 4.7. Public School Districts Served

Responses	Count	%
1	740	61.2%
2	277	23.0%
3	110	9.1%
4	52	4.3%
5	11	0.9%
6	5	0.4%
7 or more	14	1.1%
Total responses	1,209	100%

STATES IN WHICH RESPONDENTS WERE EMPLOYED AS SUPERINTENDENTS

Research has shown that there are two primary factors that have made it less complicated for superintendents to work in multiple states during their careers: early retirement provisions in state pension funds and increased licensing reciprocity (Kowalski and Sweetland, 2005). In this study, 90.7% of superintendents report serving as a superintendent in only *one* state and 7.9% in *two* states. In the 2010 study 9.5% reported serving in *two* states. All responses concerning the number of states served are in table 4.8.

Table 4.8. Number of States Serving as a Superintendent

Responses	Count	%
1	1,097	90.7%
2	96	7.9%
3	11	0.9%
4	2	0.2%
5 or more	3	0.3%
Total responses	1,209	100%

EMPLOYMENT IMMEDIATELY PRIOR TO CURRENT POSITION

The 2010 study (Kowalski et al.) revealed that 33.8% of superintendents responded that they were employed in the same district when they were selected to serve as superintendent. Collectively, data in table 4.9 reveal that a slightly higher percentage (37.1%) of the superintendents who participated in this survey were hired internally.

Superintendents in districts enrolling 25,000 or more students were more likely than peers in other district enrollment categories to have been promoted internally. Generally speaking, the larger the district, the more likely the superintendent is selected from within. Unlike smaller districts, larger districts have the opportunity to groom candidates as they move through the ranks (Kowalski, 2006). One caveat here is that the number of superintendents in the sample from districts of 25,000 or more is much lower than respondents from smaller districts.

Table 4.9. Internal/External Selection of Superintendent: District Enrollment

Employed in district when selected as superintendent	Yes	No	Total
< 300	38.03%	61.97%	11.81%
300–999	31.89%	68.11%	26.87%
1,000–2,999	38.69%	61.31%	33.11%
3,000–4,999	37.27%	62.73%	9.15%
5,000–9,999	38.79%	61.21%	9.65%
10,000–24,999	38.27%	61.73%	6.74%
25,000–49,999	59.09%	40.91%	1.83%
50,000–99,999	33.33%	66.67%	0.50%
100,000 or more	75.00%	25.00%	0.33%
Total	37.1%	62.9%	100%

PRIMARY REASON FOR SELECTION

Research has demonstrated that rapidly shifting social, political, and economic trends place greater demands on superintendents for student achievement. As school effectiveness takes center stage politically and accountability has become a priority for boards of education, the employment of superintendents has become a much more public process for school boards and candidates (Petersen, 2010). The 2020 survey asked respondents to identify the primary reasons that they believe they were selected for their current position.

Disaggregated data were reported in chapter 3 related to this question. Here we present aggregate data. The most common aggregate responses to why superintendents thought they were hired was *personal characteristics,* followed by the *ability to communicate with stakeholders,* and the *ability to be an instructional leader.* Complete response data for this issue are in table 4.10. In the 2010 study (Kowalski et al.), 33.5% of superintendents said the primary factor in their employment was *personal characteristics,* an additional percentage (24.9%) said it was to be *a change agent,* and another 20% said it was to be *an instructional leader.* The results reported here are generally congruent with the 2010 study.

Table 4.10.   Reasons for Selection

Response	Count	Percentage
Ability to be a political leader on education issues	227	18.9%
Ability to be an instructional leader	694	57.8%
Ability to communicate with stakeholders	711	59.2%
Ability to maintain the status quo	45	3.7%
Ability to manage fiscal resources	536	44.6%
Ability to use/conduct research to solve problems	197	16.4%
Communication skills	618	51.5%
Having leadership/managerial experience outside of education	100	8.3%
Personal characteristics (such as integrity, honesty, tact)	914	76.1%
Potential to be a change agent	564	47.0%
Other (please specify)	54	4.5%
Total Responses	1,201	100%

Note: Multiple answers per participant possible. Percentages added may exceed 100 since a participant may select more than one answer for this question.

SUPERINTENDENT PROFILE: CAREER PLANS IN 2025

Respondents were asked to identify where they intended to be professionally in 2025. Responses are contained in table 4.11. More than half (59.5%) of the respondents intend to be superintendents in 2025. This finding is nine percentage points higher than the 2010 study (Kowalski et al.), when 50.7% of respondents planned on remaining in the superintendency within five years. This finding would suggest that while there will be a substantial number of superintendents leaving the superintendency without the intention of returning in 2025, the percentage planning to remain in the profession has risen. Of the superintendents who intend to retire by 2025 (n=*303*), 25.15% plan to continue working part-time post retirement with only 9.05% who plan to retire completely.

SUPERINTENDENT PROFILE: PLANS ON DEPARTURE

Superintendents were asked to identify what their plans were upon leaving the superintendency. Responses are contained in table 4.12. This question is new for the 2020 study. In contrast

Table 4.11. Superintendent Profile: Career Plans in 2025

Responses	Count	Percentage
Remaining in my current position	516	42.8%
Remaining a superintendent but in a different district	201	16.7%
Being a district or school administrator other than a superintendent	16	1.3%
Being a college or university professor	14	1.2%
Being a college or university administrator	4	0.3%
Being an elementary or secondary school teacher	4	0.3%
Being a full-time education consultant	19	1.6%
Being a full-time employee in a field outside education	19	1.6%
Being retired but continuing to work in some capacity on a part-time basis	303	25.1%
Being retired and not employed in any capacity	109	9.1%
Total Responses	1,205	100%

Table 4.12. Superintendent Profile: Plans upon Departure

Responses	Count	Percentage
Enjoy my leisure time	874	72.6%
Teach college-level courses	471	39.2%
Work as an administrator at a local college	84	7.0%
Become a consultant to local school districts or superintendents	684	57.0%
Work for a professional education association	204	16.9%
Seek a second career in another industry/outside education	387	32.2%
Work in educational technology	38	3.2%
Write articles or a book about my experiences in education	174	14.5%
Total Unique Responses	1,203	
Total Responses	2,916	

Note: Multiple answers per participant possible. Percentages added may exceed 100 since a participant may select more than one answer for this question.

to superintendent career plans for 2025 (table 4.10), in which only 1.16% said they would want to be a college or university professor, 39.2% of respondents in the 2020 study indicated that they want to teach college level courses when they leave the superintendency.

Responses also provide insight into what other work superintendents are contemplating once they leave the superintendency. Fifty-seven percent want to be consultants and 32.2% plan on starting a second career. Given that 72.6% wish to enjoy their leisure time and given that respondents could select up to three choices, the profile of retired superintendents appears to be one where superintendents plan to work part-time but able to enjoy their leisure time upon retirement.

CONCLUSION

We began this chapter with the hypothesis that the unprecedented changes in K–12 education would have an impact on the career pathways of superintendents of schools. The data in this investigation do not bear out this hypothesis and we are left to wonder why.

In general, we found the responses to our questions have reinforced our understanding of how superintendents access their first superintendency, their experiences once in the role, and their future plans upon stepping away. We see that in the last decade the professional experiences of teaching and serving as a school principal remain the traditional career trajectory for superintendents. We also found that educational levels and areas of academic focus and preparation have not changed since the 2010 study.

The data also indicated that the professional experiences of superintendents and the number of states and districts served remain consistent over the past decade, with a majority of superintendents serving in only one or two districts and in one state. Superintendent employment and selection has not really changed over the last ten years. Consistent with the findings in the 2010 study, results from this investigation demonstrate that superintendents in larger and more urban districts with 25,000 or more students are more likely than peers in other district enrollment categories to be promoted internally. We also see that the superintendents in the 2020 study listed *personal characteristics* as the number one reason they were hired. This is similar to the 2010 study, followed by the *ability to communicate with stakeholders* and the *ability to be an instructional leader*.

Finally, respondents were also asked to identify where they intended to be professionally in 2025. Results pointed to the fact that a majority intended on remaining in the superintendency at least for the next five years. The 2020 study asked a new question about the future plans of superintendents once they retired. Three-quarters expressed a desire to enjoy their leisure time, while a little over half expressing an interest in becoming consultants and almost one-third said they plan on starting a second career.

So, why was there not a significant change in the career pathways of superintendents? After all, the same cannot be said for the teaching profession. Large-scale, top-down education reform combined with deteriorating salaries and working conditions impacted the daily lives of teachers through this past decade. The number of college-educated individuals entering teacher preparation programs has declined precipitously in the last decade as the profession has become marginally less attractive than other employment (King and Hampel, 2018). Compounding this issue is that nearly 8% of teachers have left the profession over the last ten years (Darling-Hammond and Carver-Thomas, 2016). During this same period, master's programs in education that often lead to initial principal certification have also experienced declines in enrollment. This is not surprising when the same factors impacting teachers' work lives have impacted educational leaders' lives as well (U.S. Department of Education, 2018).

Although we do not see the same changes in the career paths of superintendents of schools, perhaps the simplest explanation is that superintendents are at the end of the career pipeline—and the teacher and principal shortages are yet to work their way through to the top of the organization. At the outset we thought we might have seen, for example, superintendents changing positions more frequently as they are forced to cope with increased demands to affect educational improvement and declining real resources (Baker, 2018). Like teacher education, we were also inclined to think there might be a proliferation in non-traditional career paths into the superintendency as districts seek to expand the pool of qualified superintendents. Based on the changes in education, we also thought we might have seen superintendents taking positions at even younger ages as opportunities arise, especially in smaller districts. Yet we did not see any of these trends in our data.

Our data confirms that most superintendents still work their way from teacher to principal to central office en route to the top. As those willing to begin that journey shrink in number, we are left to wonder if the remarkable changes in other parts of the profession will impact the career pathways of superintendents by the next iteration of this study in 2030.

REFERENCES

Baker, B. D. (2018). *Educational Inequality and School Finance*. Cambridge: Harvard Education Press.

Callan, M. F., and Levinson, W. (2011). *Achieving Success for New and Aspiring Superintendents: A Practical Guide*. Thousand Oaks, CA: Corwin.

Darling-Hammond, L., and Carver-Thomas, D. (2016, September). *A Coming Crisis in Teaching? Teacher Supply, Demand and Shortages in the U.S.* Washington, DC: Learning Policy Institute.

Glass, T. E., Björk, L., and Brunner, C. C. (2000). *The Study of the American School Superintendency, 2000: A Look at the Superintendent of Education in the New Millennium*. Arlington, VA: American Association of School Administrators.

King, J. E., and Hampel, R. (2018). *Colleges of Education: A National Portrait*. Washington, DC: American Association of Colleges of Teacher Education.

Kowalski, T. J., (2006). *The School Superintendent: Theory, Practice, and Cases* (2nd ed.) Thousand Oaks, CA: Sage.

Kowalski, T. J., McCord, R. S., Petersen, G. J., Young, P. I. and Ellerson, N. M. (2010). *The American School Superintendent: 2010 Decennial Study*. Arlington, VA: American Association of School Administrators.

Kowalski, T. J., and Sweetland, S. R., (2005). "Retire-Rehire Policy in State Pension Programs for School Administrators." *Planning and Changing* 36 (1/2), 3–22.

Heneman, H. G., Judge, T. A., and Kammeyer-Muller, J. (2018). *Staffing Organizations* (9th ed.). New York: McGraw Hill Education.

Petersen, G. J. (2010). "At the Epicenter of Educational Change: Challenges and the Role of Professional Development for Executive Leaders." In S. Conley and B. S. Cooper (Eds.), *Preparing Tomorrow's School Leaders: Growth and Life Cycle Approaches* (pp. 171–95). Lanham, MD: Rowman & Littlefield Education.

U.S. Department of Education, National Center for Education Statistics, Higher Education General Information Survey (HEGIS). (2018). *"Degrees and Other Formal Awards Conferred" Surveys, 1970–71 through 1985–86; Integrated Postsecondary Education Data System (IPEDS), "Completions Survey" (IPEDS-C:91–99); and IPEDS Fall 2000 through Fall 2017*. Washington, DC.

Chapter Five

The Current Work of the American Superintendent

Gregory C. Hutchings Jr. and John L. Brown

The current work of the superintendent is evolving from earlier models associated with technical-managerial approaches toward adaptive leadership approaches (Heifetz, Grashow, and Linsky, 2009; Kowalski, McCord, Petersen, Young, and Ellerson, 2010). Increasingly, the modern superintendent must be a communicator, a facilitator of adult and student learning, a collaborator, and a change agent. The superintendent must be able to mobilize diverse groups with sometimes diverse opinions and goals, and bring them together to confront tough issues in ways that facilitate education equity for all students.

The respondents surveyed for this study universally confirmed that the contemporary role of superintendent is a challenging one, and it requires an individual who understands the power of professional learning, the necessity of data-driven approaches to addressing problems of practice, and the significance of distributed leadership to ensure that educators and stakeholders within a school district receive multiple opportunities to express their personal voice and engage actively in decision-making and problem-solving processes (Darling-Hammond, Flook, Cook-Harvey, Barron, Osher, 2019; Adams, 2014; Fullan, 2005).

The challenges and opportunities presented by the role of superintendent also require prospective and in-service leaders to understand the scope and dimensions of the changing demographic landscape evident in all schools throughout the United States. Growing levels of racial and ethnic diversity require superintendents to support the educators they lead to understand the influence of diversity on education. Superintendents must also understand the influence of diversity on the "whole child" approach to education. The current work of superintendents requires the application of skills, knowledge, and dispositions aimed at holistically addressing the student's cognitive, social-emotional, and physical needs and developmental processes (Daggett, 2016; Darling-Hammond et al., 2019; Jones and Kahn, 2017; National Academies of Sciences, Engineering, and Medicine, 2018).

The modern superintendent must be an instructional leader who embraces and articulates the range of insights about the learning process associated with neuroscience brain-based research, cognitive learning theory, culturally relevant pedagogy, and constructivist models of education, as well as what Daggett (2016) and others emphasized as the need for "trauma-skilled schools." Superintendents are increasingly confronted with the need to incorporate current research conclusions about the impact of traumatic life events and living conditions upon students and the effects of short- and long-term trauma upon student achievement, grade retention, overall health and well-being, and graduation rates.

PURPOSE

This chapter explores participants' responses from the 2020 AASA Decennial Study of the Superintendent national survey as they pertain to the current work of the superintendent. The section provides insights into the impact of the changing American landscape upon the work of public education's leaders. Survey respondents were generally in agreement about the importance of addressing the differing needs, backgrounds, cultural traditions, and readiness levels evident among increasingly diverse student populations. Over the course of the chapter, we present results from the survey participants' and recommendations concerning the following key meta-themes and organizing themes:

The Changing Profile of School Districts: This first section explores how diverse student populations present increasingly complex needs and learner profiles that successful educational leaders, especially superintendents, must recognize and address.

The Joys and Areas of Fulfillment of Superintendents: This section investigated the positive side of district leadership, reinforcing the implicit and explicit motivational factors that give superintendents a sense of achievement and pride in their role as district leader.

The Greatest Problems Facing Superintendents of Public Schools: The third section explores the universal challenges confronting individuals in the role of superintendent in contemporary school districts, including the paradigm shift from technical-managerial approaches toward adaptive leadership with the superintendent assuming the roles of collaborative problem solver, decision maker, and instructional leader.

Issues Consuming the Most Time for Superintendents: A variation of the third meta-theme of problems confronting leadership is time consumption. Time, or the lack thereof, appears to be a significant concern for most survey respondents.

Strategies for Addressing the Most Pressing Identified Problems: This section highlights recommendations and continuing concerns associated with problems related to district-level leadership practice.

Stresses Felt in the Role of Superintendent: The survey revealed universal agreement that being a superintendent necessitates the individual's confrontation of both external problems requiring sometimes immediate solutions and internal stresses that can diminish the leader's healthy sense of well-being and work-life balance.

Skills Areas Most in Need of Improvement among Superintendents: This honest and revealing section of the survey allowed respondents to declare those areas in which they perceive themselves as adult learners requiring further professional growth and development.

Leading Conversations about Race and Equity in the District and Community: A key aspect of leadership is the necessity of conducting courageous conversations about the impact of race and racism upon student achievement, social and emotional development, and overall sense of efficacy and well-being. This section provides insights about how superintendents address this significant national issue.

The Role and Importance of School Boards Leading Equity Conversations: Respondents were consistently clear about the importance of equity as a key component of discourse in their schools and districts. This section explores respondents' insights concerning their relationship with their School Boards—and the necessity of equity conversations as a sustained part of governance and oversight.

CHANGING PROFILE OF SCHOOL DISTRICTS

School districts are evolving throughout the United States in terms of diversity of demographics, changing learner needs, and an increasing commitment to addressing the needs of the "whole child." Specifically, district leaders demonstrate awareness that learning is a constructivist process in which the student interacts with the teacher, the content, and peers to make sense of content and move increasingly toward growing levels of independent application and autonomous use of skills, knowledge, and understandings (Mortensen, 2008; National Academies of Sciences, Engineering, and Medicine, 2018).

The growing linguistic and socioeconomic diversity of districts (College Board Advocacy and Policy Center, 2010) requires superintendents to have some understanding of instructional leadership and culturally relevant pedagogy (Ladson-Billings, 1995; Tatum, 1999; Terrell and Lindsey, 2009). Additionally, school district leaders are responsible for building professional learning communities designed to purposefully use data, in all its forms, to address emerging and long-standing problems of practice. Perhaps most significantly, the superintendent must serve as a vision and mission keeper, someone who models and reinforces values related to high expectations, educational equity, and diversity (Senge, 2012).

JOYS AND AREAS OF FULFILLMENT OF THE SUPERINTENDENT

For many superintendents surveyed for this publication, joy and fulfillment come from ensuring that education is results-driven and student-focused. Superintendents expressed fulfillment when they established a coherent and aligned strategic plan and demonstrated progress toward achieving identified targets. Instructional leaders derive joy from observing students who are enjoying and are deeply engaged in the learning process (Harvey, Cambron-McCabe, Cunningham, and Koff, 2013; Lindsey, Robins, and Terrell, 2009; Darling-Hammond and Rothman, 2017).

The extant literature suggests that one way superintendents experience fulfillment with the role is when they observe and receive feedback from teachers who are growing in their understanding of what they are doing in the classroom. They also experience fulfillment when the vision and mission of the school district, as well as core values, are operationalized in the various learning environments of the school district (Harvey et al., 2013). Successful superintendents understand, model, and support evidence-based best practices in the areas of teaching, learning, assessment, and classroom management (National Academies of Sciences, Engineering, and Medicine, 2018).

PROBLEMS FACING SUPERINTENDENTS OF PUBLIC SCHOOLS

To use a cliché with great value, a problem is an opportunity disguised as a challenge. The data generated from this survey suggests that one of the greatest problems facing public school leaders is that politicians and competing political perspectives hamper the ability of public education to achieve its full potential as an equalizer designed to promote the achievement of diverse learners. Consequently, superintendents face increasing levels of rhetoric degrading or critiquing public education, frequently resulting in the elimination or diversion of funding to support equitable public education (Harvey, Cambron-McCabe, Cunningham, and Koff, 2013).

For example, family services outside of school hours, social and emotional services for students, summer enrichment and intervention programs, universal preschool, career development options, and mental and physical health management are frequently being diminished or underfunded. Additionally, there needs to be increasing support, understanding, and funding for what Daggett (2016) referred to as "trauma-skilled schools." Trauma-skilled schools provide learning environments that recognize the impact of trauma upon learners—and provide classroom-based and school-based support and interventions to ameliorate its effects upon student achievement and well-being (Gailer and Dunlap, 2018; Daggett, 2016).

Superintendents responded that they are aware the pipeline for entrance into education as a profession is narrowing, especially for teachers of color. State and federal policies are inadvertently diminishing the attitudes and perspectives of teachers and future teachers about the value of the profession. The negative perspectives of some current and future educators are influenced in part by the general perceptions that educators are underpaid for the amount of work they do and the conditions in which they work can be challenging. A growing challenge has become finding ways to address the increasing numbers of students who suffer from differing degrees of trauma and lack of social and emotional support (Daggett, 2016; Gates, Baird, Master, and Chavez-Herrerias, 2019).

The current anti–public school political environment and deteriorating societal conditions require expanded leadership ingenuity and creativity to engage people in the field of education as a career pathway open to them. Frequently, educators themselves can be their own worst critics, reinforcing the negative aspects of their profession rather than touting it as the great gateway for supporting individuals to enter and succeed in the world. Superintendents need to model and reinforce the prestige, value, and enduring impact of education as a career avenue (Adams, 2014; College Board Advocacy and Policy Center, 2010; Durlak, Weissberg, Dymnicki, Taylor, and Schellinger, 2011; Harvey et al., 2013).

ISSUES CONSUMING THE MOST TIME FOR SUPERINTENDENTS

According to the survey data, financial issues, personnel management, conflict management, and school board relations are the most time-consuming issue facing the superintendent (see figure 5.1). Fiscal stewardship is identified as the most critical area facing the superintendent since they are expected to be responsible with local, state, and federal tax dollars. School districts compete with other organizations and agencies for funding within urban, suburban, and rural districts.

Expectations continue to increase, while unfortunately, participants indicated that adequate funding is more difficult to attain as a result of a growing number of unfunded mandates and social issues, including poverty, that require increased resource allocation. This phenomenon can result in underachievement of learners and morale issues confronting staff. Superintendents must be savvy financial managers and balance the educational wants and needs of students, staff, parents, and the local community with the financial realities of shrinking school funding (Gates et al., 2019; Education Writers Association, 2003; Darling Hammond et al., 2019).

The second most time-consuming issue involves personnel and conflict management, including collective bargaining. Superintendents are forced into the collective bargaining arena and try to balance relationships, what is best for the organization, and financial decision making within difficult fiscal conditions. In effect, the superintendent must be skilled at realizing that this process results in the perception that somebody is "losing" while someone else is winning. This process is a human relations issue as much as a financial one. An effective superintendent must have active listening and communication skills to intervene when conflicts arise and feelings are hurt (Durlak et al., 2011; Fullan, 2005; Senge, 2012).

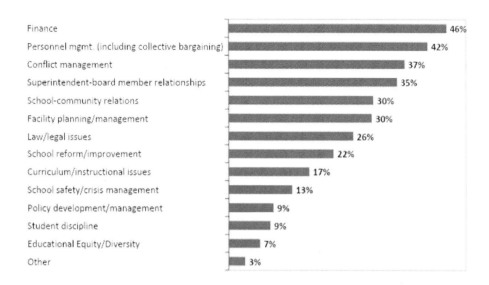

Figure 5.1.   Issues Consuming Superintendents' Time.

Conflict management is an essential leadership skill. Some superintendents manage hundreds to thousands of staff who demonstrate a wide range of work styles, attitudes, and skill levels. Superintendents must be effective facilitators of the change process, whether at the macro or micro levels. Participants responded that an effective superintendent must be able to understand the impact of conflict upon individuals and groups, recognize the need to be facilitators of problem-solving and decision-making processes, and demonstrate emotional intelligence while managing diverse personalities and conflicting perspectives. Participants' responses painted a picture of a leader who must facilitate change while striving to maintain stability and equilibrium within the organization (Terrell and Lindsey, 2009; Wheatley, 2002).

Another common issue that consumes the time of superintendents is board of education relations. Effective superintendents work collaboratively with their school boards. The major issue with establishing such relationships, however, is the continual change evident among board personnel and superintendents. Frequently, the turnover process among board members and within the superintendency results in school districts failing to get traction in attaining strategic planning goals or ensuring continual improvement toward the process of achieving designated performance targets (Senge, 2012; Harvey et al., 2013).

School boards throughout the United States struggle to understand their role as a governing body, with constant tugs-of-war between the superintendent and board members concerning how best to implement and monitor the district's strategic plan. Board members can sometimes "get into the weeds," overreaching into areas of personnel management, instructional programming, and day-to-day operations (Daggett, 2016; Adams, 2014).

The result is that some districts experience a lack of cohesive vision, mission, and core values. In light of competing roles among board members and superintendents, staff members also face challenges in understanding specific expectations and professional guidance and requirements of the organization. The most effective school districts have superintendents who understand their role as the chief executive officer and boards who understand their role as the governing body of the school district (Harvey et al., 2013; Education Writers Association, 2003; Gates et al., 2019).

One interesting finding is that superintendents indicated that educational equity and diversity are the least time-consuming issues. It is impossible to know from the data why equity and diversity rated so low as a time-consuming issue given how participants and the existing literature highlight the impact of the changing cultural and racial demographics of America's schools. Issues of equity are explored in other chapters of this study and those findings, along with the findings reported here, suggest that equity might be an area in which the profession has not yet caught up with the identification of the many equity and diversity-oriented issues that need to be addressed

STRATEGIES FOR ADDRESSING THE MOST PRESSING PROBLEMS

The most pressing problem confronting superintendents, according to the survey data, involves job-related stress (see figure 5.2). There was almost universal agreement that the job of superintendent is stressful. Specifically, for the superintendent, the position is a 24-hour-a-day job. Superintendents are constantly "on" and they are required to give of themselves on a constant basis in many forums. The superintendent is ultimately "where the buck stops," and superintendents indicated that they are responsible for all systemic outcomes and results. The leader is constantly managing the change process, from board members' concerns to student needs to community trends (Senge, 2012; Terrell and Lindsey, 2009; Harvey et al., 2019; Gailer and Dunlap, 2018).

According to data, the second most pressing problem involves time requirements for the superintendents. They are expected to attend a range of meetings, including public and private board meeting sessions, community groups, athletics events and student performances, and other types of presentations. The challenges and the demands upon time are never-ending. As what is essentially *the chief executive officer* of a major organization, superintendents must become effective at oversight and development of annual budgets, physical plant operations,

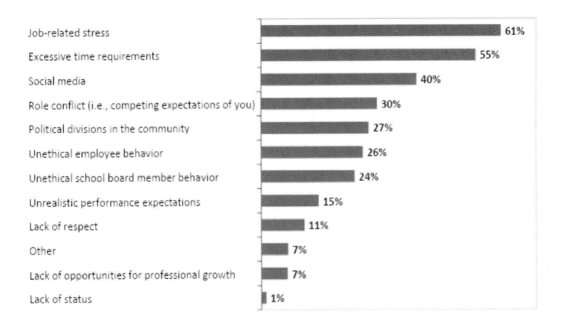

Figure 5.2.   Problems Facing Superintendents in Their Current Positions.

and quality control in all aspects of the organization (Adams, 2014; Education Writers Association, 2003).

The third most pressing problem that superintendents brought out is that they must understand and respond to social media in its varied forms. Both the district leader and his or her communications' office or designee must continually be available to monitor and respond to social media. Every individual who has a cell phone or other technology-based device is becoming a reporter. A minor incident can "go viral" quickly and force the superintendent and/or leadership team to address incidents quickly and effectively to avoid a firestorm of negative attention. Superintendents are expected to be "media-ready" at all times and are expected to have a social media presence (Carvill, 2018; Mortensen, 2008; Price, 2013).

STRESSES FELT BY SUPERINTENDENTS

A sizable majority of the responding superintendents indicated that finding a sustainable work-life balance is challenging. Only 8% of respondents indicated that they felt *little* or *no* stress as a superintendent whereas 56% *felt very great* or *considerable* stress. The remaining 36% of the respondents felt *moderate* stress. The stress factor is of great concern since a wide range of research studies confirm that without this balance, individuals are subject to higher degrees of physical stress, medical issues, and challenges in sustaining effective relationships with family and friends (Gailer and Dunlap, 2018).

Superintendents must be intentional and conscious about spending time with family and friends, addressing their physical and psychological well-being (e.g., routine physicals, workout sessions, healthy food options, ensuring proper nutrition), and accessing appropriate medical or psychological services as needed. Stress is inevitable in the role of the superintendent; therefore, the individual in that role must be conscious of the need for balance. Additionally, the effective superintendent takes advantage of advice, executive coaching, and support from fellow superintendents (Harvey et al., 2013).

AREAS FOR GROWTH FOR SUPERINTENDENTS

The data suggest that the skill most in need of growth is leading social and emotional learning (see figure 5.3). Some students have encountered adverse childhood experiences associated with trauma, whether through a single incident, over time, or through association with the growing presence of conflict on social media or living in impoverished conditions.

Superintendents must be equipped to address the trauma-related challenges facing students and those who teach them, whether academic, social, emotional, or physical (Gailer and Dunlap, 2018; Jones and Kahn, 2017; Tatum, 1999). Daggett (2016) emphasized the need for educational leaders to support educators to become "trauma-skilled" and capable of providing support and interventions within the classroom and school building. Superintendents need to be able to provide the leadership necessary to help educators address students suffering from the after-effects of traumatic incidents and traumatic environmental conditions (Daggett, 2016).

Superintendents should be familiar with social and emotional learning theories and practices and the ways to instill those practices into learning organizations (Harvey, Cambron-McCabe, Cunningham, and Koff, 2013; National Academies of Sciences, Engineering, and Medicine, 2018). Superintendents need to build the capacity of their staff and become competent in leading the development of trauma-informed strategies that build a sense of community, student voice, and a sense of connectedness to the school. Such strategies reinforce the

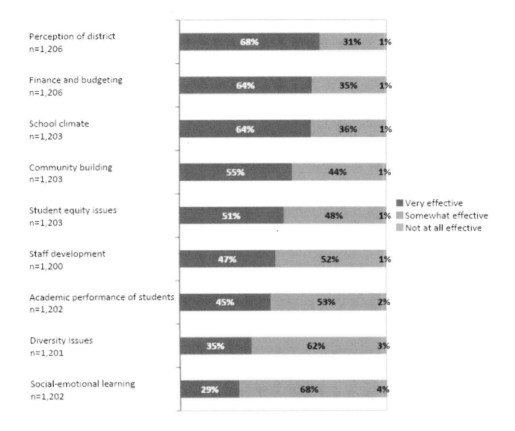

Figure 5.3. Skills Most in Needed for Growth.

ability of the learner to interact with others, self-monitor, resolve conflicts, and work success-fully as part of a team (Darling-Hammond and Rothman, 2017; Harvey et al., 2013; Jones and Kahn, 2017).

Finally, the education equity, or the lack thereof for some groups of students, is an essential issue faced by superintendents. A majority of respondents indicated they do not feel well prepared to lead discussions on equity. Equity involves a superintendent's commitment to ensure that all students are provided not only the resources they need for a comprehensive education, but the supports necessary to make the most of those resources.

Access to resources is not enough in terms of educational equity. Some students, because of issues outside of their control, cannot make full use of the resources to which they are provided access (Scherrer, 2014). Equity requires that students' academic, social, and emotional needs are met where they are, not where a distal policy-making force thinks they should be. Superintendents must lead for equity on behalf of students to ensure that all students can progress meaningfully toward achieving their innate potential in post-secondary education and the various career pathways (Tatum, 1999; Terrell and Lindsey, 2009).

A strong majority of superintendents (89%) who responded to the survey indicated that conversations about race within their community were an *extremely important* or an *important* factor in ensuring student progress and success whereas 11% responded that such conversations were not important. However, most indicated that they were underprepared to lead these discussions. The lack of expertise on leading discussions about race and equity among superintendents represents a challenge for school district leaders across the United States as they struggle to address the root causes of academic, social, and emotional difficulties for students.

Professional learning providers and professional associations should consider the results reported here and engage with superintendents regarding their needs for training on issues of equity and race. Specifically, the results suggest that superintendents want to focus on strategies to help them navigate and lead discussions about race within their communities. Likewise, boards of education and their professional associations should invest in policies and training supports that focus on equity and race to ensure that board of education officials receive the professional learning they need to collaborate with superintendents and support them as they address equity issues (Harvey et al., 2013; Lindsey, Robins, and Terrell, 2009).

Superintendents must strive to support their districts in overcoming obstacles related to equity. Research confirms that schools across the United States are more segregated than they were prior to the *Brown v. Board of Education* decision. Neighborhoods across America are just as segregated as they were during the Civil Rights Movement. According to many contemporary researchers, most school districts today have neighborhood schools that reflect the de-facto segregation of students within neighborhoods. School board policies also perpetuate segregation within schools via policies like tracking, ability-level grouping, and unconscious forms of socioeconomic grouping and segregation via reliance on results from standardized tests to make important grouping decisions about students (College Board Advocacy and Policy Center, 2010; Tienken, 2020).

Superintendents must be innovative in their approaches to providing a more integrated learning experience for all students, regardless of their zip code, background, academic readiness, or socioeconomic status. This process is essential if equity and success for all students is to become a reality rather than an aspiration. This is one of the most difficult tasks facing the United States, which in turn, becomes one of the most difficult tasks facing the nation's superintendents (Mortensen, 2008; Rodela and Bertrand, 2018).

THE IMPORTANCE OF SCHOOL BOARDS LEADING EQUITY CONVERSATIONS

A majority of superintendents who engaged in conversations about equity indicated that they led those conversations (see figure 5.4). Respondents indicated that their boards of education did not facilitate or lead conversations about equity. One conclusion we make based on the results is that these conversations should be co-facilitated by superintendents, school board officials, community leaders, and staff, as well as the community. The stakeholder groups must be directly involved in co-facilitation in order to have a true and enduring impact upon the organization culture and practices of the district (Senge, 2012; Daggett, 2018; Jencks and Phillips, 1998).

The implication of this conclusion reinforces the recurrent themes evident in this survey data, including the importance of the superintendent as initiator, discourse facilitator, and networker, the value of crucial conversations about significant issues affecting student achievement, and the critical value of the superintendent as a facilitator of the change process. The importance of equity conversations led collaboratively by the school board and the superintendent is highly aligned with Wallace Foundation and Education Writers Association (2003, p. 6) conclusions about the essentials of leadership and board interface, including the following:

- Shared commitment to improving the achievement of all students
- Collaborative discourse related to student achievement and well-being

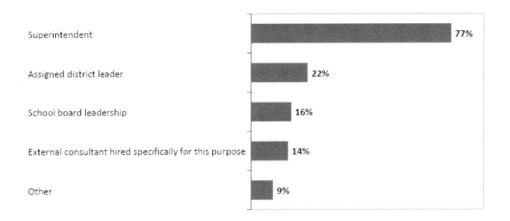

Figure 5.4.   Leaders of Conversations Related to Issues of Equity.

- The necessity of the board working through the superintendent to represent the whole district, displaying openness with the community in decision making

CONCLUSION

As the above data suggest, respondents generally agree that these are challenging but exciting times to be a superintendent. The responses reveal several key meta-themes that appear to have universal relevance to superintendents:

- schools and districts require visionary and mission-driven leadership to support staff in responding to the needs of increasingly diverse student populations;
- the position of superintendent offers a range of areas for joy, celebration, and fulfillment related to student progress and move toward success in post-secondary education and career pathway options;
- challenges confronting superintendents include time constraints, changing instructional paradigms, conflicting stakeholder perspectives, the influence of social media and technology, and competing demands for time and resources;
- superintendents understand that it is important to be collaborative with staff and to form and sustain professional learning communities that dignify the voices and perspectives of stakeholders to confront the various challenges they face in the position; and
- respondents reinforced the necessity for superintendents to initiate courageous conversations about race and equity with all stakeholders as an essential component of governance and district oversight.

Without question, it takes hard work, commitment, and principled dedication to assume and sustain the role of the superintendent in our change-dominated and technology-driven world. Respondents confirmed that if superintendents make building the professional capacity of educational leaders a priority in their current work and unapologetically tackle inequities confronting schools across the United States, public schools will ensure a brighter future for the next generation.

REFERENCES

Adams, S. (November 12, 2014). "The Ten Skills Employers Most Want in 2015 Graduates." *Forbes.* Retrieved from https://www.forbes.com/sites/susanadams/2014/11/12/the-10-skills-employers-most-want-in-2015-graduates/#d9a90ec25116.

Carvill, M. (2018). *Get Social: Social Media Strategies and Tactics for Leaders.* Great Britain and New York: Kogan Page Limited.

College Board Advocacy and Policy Center. (2010). *The Educational Crisis Facing Young Men of Color.* New York: College Board.

Daggett, W. R. (2016). *Making Schools Work: A Vision for College and Career Ready Learning.* New York: Math Solutions.

Daggett, W. R. (2018). *Rigor and Relevance from Concept to Reality.* New York: Instructional Center for Leadership in Education.

Darling-Hammond, L., Flook, L., Cook-Harvey, C., Barron, B., and Osher, D. (2019). "Implications for Practice of the Science of Learning and Development." *Applied Developmental Science.* DOI: 10.1080/10888691.2018.1537791

Darling-Hammond, L., and Rothman, R. (2017). *Teaching in a Flat World: Learning from High-Performing Systems.* New York: Teachers College Press.

Durlak, J., Weissberg, R., Dymnicki, A., Taylor, R., and Schellinger, K. (2011). "The Impact of Enhancing Students' Social and Emotional Learning: A Meta-Analysis of School-Based Universal Interventions," *Child Development* 82 (1), 405–432.

Education Writers Association. (2003). EWA Special Report: *Effective Superintendents, Effective Boards: Finding the Right Fit.* Washington, DC: The Wallace Foundation.

Fullan, M. (2005). *Leadership and Sustainability: Systems Thinkers in Action.* Thousand Oaks, CA: Corwin Press.

Gailer, J., S. Addis, and Dunlap, L. (2018). *Improving School Outcomes for Trauma-Impact Students.* Anderson, SC: National Dropout Prevention Center and Successful Practices Network.

Gates, S. M., Baird, M. D. Master, B. K., and Chavez-Herrerias, E. R. (2019). *Principal Pipelines: A Feasible, Affordable, and Effective Way for Districts to Improve Schools.* Santa Monica, CA: Rand Corp.

Harvey, J., Cambron-McCabe, N., Cunningham, L. L., and Koff, R. H. (2013). *The Superintendent's Fieldbook: A Guide for Leaders of Learning* (2nd ed.). Thousand Oaks, CA: Corwin.

Heifetz, R. A., Grashow, A., and Linsky, M. (2009). *The Practice of Adaptive Leadership: Tools and Tactics for Changing Your Organization and the World.* Boston: Harvard Business Press.

Jencks, C., and Phillips, M. (Eds.). (1998). *The Black-White Test Score Gap.* Washington, DC: Brookings Institute.

Jones, S., and Kahn, J. (2017). *The Evidence Base for How We Learn: Supporting Students' Social, Emotional, and Academic Development: Consensus Statements of Evidence from the Council of Distinguished Scientists.* Washington, DC: The Aspen Institute National Commission on Social, Emotional, and Academic Development.

Kowalski, T. J., McCord, R. S., Petersen, G. J, Young, I. P., and Ellerson, N. M. (2010). *The American School Superintendent: 2010 Decennial Study.* Lanham, MD: Rowman and Littlefield.

Ladson-Billings, G. (1995). "Toward a Theory of Culturally Relevant Pedagogy. *American Education Research Journal* 32 (3), 465–91.

Lindsey, R., Robins, K., and Terrell, R. (2009) *Cultural Proficiency: A Manual for School Leaders.* Thousand Oaks, CA: Corwin Press.

Mortensen, T. G. (2008, Number 196). *Educational Attainment and Economic Welfare, 1940 to 2008.* Oskaloosa, IA: Postsecondary Education Opportunity.

National Academies of Sciences, Engineering, and Medicine. (2018). *How People Learn II: Learners, Contexts, and Cultures.* Washington, DC: The National Academies Press.

Price, D. (2013). *How We'll Work, Live and Learn in the Future.* England: Crux.

Rodela, K. C., and Bertrand, M. (2018). "Rethinking Educational Leadership in the Margins: Youth, Parent, and Community Leadership for Equity and Social Justice." *Journal of Research on Leadership Education* 13 (1), 3–9. https://doi.org/10.1177/1942775117751306

Scherrer, J. (2014). "The Role of the Intellectual in Eliminating Poverty: A Response to Tierney." *Educational Researcher* 43, 201–7.

Senge, P. (2012). *Schools That Learn: A Fifth Discipline Fieldbook for Educators, Parents, and Everyone Who Cares about Education.* New York: Crown Press.

Tatum, B. D. (1999). *Why Are All the Black Kids Sitting Together in the Cafeteria?* New York: Basic Books.

Terrell, R., and Lindsey, R. (2009). *Culturally Proficient Leadership: The Personal Journey Begins Within.* Thousand Oaks, CA: Corwin Press.

Tienken, C. H. (2020). *Cracking the Code of Education Reform: Creative Compliance and Ethical Leadership.* Thousand Oaks, CA: Corwin Press.

Wheatley, M. (2002). *Turning to One Another: Simple Conversations to Restore Hope to the Future.* San Francisco: Berrett-Koehler.

Chapter Six

Professional Learning of the Superintendent

Sally Zepeda, Mary Lynne Derrington, Wendy Robinson, Sevda Yildirim, and Salih Cevik

Superintendents play a critical and complex role in leading a school district's continuous improvement efforts. Their preparation to lead is essential to supporting increased student learning and educational reform (Björk, Browne-Ferrigno, and Kowalski, 2014). Preparation before becoming a superintendent is often driven by state licensure requirements or shaped by university doctoral programs, although neither involves uniform requirements across the United States. Licensure is established and maintained by individual states; thus, criteria across the country vary (Perry, 2013; Petersen, Fusarelli, and Kowalski, 2008).

PURPOSE

The chapter examines data from the 2020 AASA study related to superintendent preparation, executive coaching, professional learning, and decision making. The literature is pervasive that professional learning for teachers, leaders, and other school personnel is more effective when it is embedded in the complexities of the work (Zepeda, 2019a; Zepeda, Jimenez, and Lanoue, 2015). Arar and Avidov-Ungar (2019) suggest that for superintendents to be able to lead their own learning, they must be able to "construct a continuous learning framework along their professional career" (p. 1). A personal learning framework is essential because what superintendents must learn changes over time based on their experiences and the multiple demands to keep pace with constantly changing needs of students and the communities in which they reside.

OVERVIEW OF PREPARATION

Unfortunately, research about the professional learning needs of superintendents has been slow to emerge (Hanover Research, 2014; Spanneut, Tobin, and Ayers, 2011) with more written about building-level leaders and teachers (Bredeson, Klar, and Johnsson, 2009; Honig and Rainey, 2014). If the aspiration is to build professional learning for superintendents that addresses their present career stage, then opportunities must follow the course of being job-embedded—relevant, timely, sustained over time, and focused on the development and refinement of practice (Zepeda, 2019b).

Doctoral and other degree programs may be considered preparation for the superintendency; however, in most districts, a doctoral degree is not required. With such variation in preparation, it is problematic to view all school leadership programs the same (Kowalski, 2013). Furthermore, doctoral programs for superintendency preparation vary; many educational leadership and administration programs do not adequately prepare candidates because little coursework is specific to the position (Kowalski, 2013; Tripses, Hunt, and Watkins, 2013).

Researchers have identified problems with the doctorate as preparation for the superintendency. Those problems include irrelevant curriculum, unsuitable research requirements inapplicable to the work of leaders, and absence of a clinical component (Levine, 2005; Shulman, Golde, Bueschel, and Garabedian, 2006). Striving to address this theory-practice gap in doctorate programs, the Carnegie Project on the Educational Doctorate (CPED, 2009) was established with the goal of developing scholarly practitioners who can apply research skills to solving problems superintendents typically encounter. Responding to the perceived disconnect between theory and practice, program providers also revised the curriculum to address skills and competencies necessary for superintendents (Hollingworth, Sullivan, Condon, Bhatt, and Brandt, 2012; Perry, 2013).

Building superintendent skills and competencies prior to and after attaining the position might be a focus of executive coaching. Executive coaching evolved over the past thirty years in business and industry, most notably provided to CEOs and other corporate echelon leaders. Executive coaching—not to be used interchangeably with other forms of coaching as in peer, and so on—is significantly different because it is a "one-to-one learning and development *intervention* that uses a collaborative, reflective, goal-focused relationship to achieve professional outcomes" (Jones, Woods, and Guillaume, 2016, p. 250; emphasis added).

The literature on executive coaching brings forward that interventions primarily serve to address system culture (Athanasopoulou and Dopson, 2018); to develop an in-house pipeline of executive level talent to support leadership succession efforts (Zepeda, Bengtson, and Parylo, 2012); to support executive leaders transition to and learn from the work within the context of the organization (DiGirolamo, 2015; Ennis and Otto, 2015); and to assist executives as they "build effective teams and deliver on organisational goals during periods of disruptive change or organisational turbulence" (Grant, 2014, p. 259).

ACADEMIC PREPARATION

This section examines superintendents' perceptions about the (1) importance of academic courses in preparing for the superintendency; (2) effectiveness of academic preparation programs; and (3) professors' credibility in educational administration/leadership courses.

The first part of this analysis explores the importance of academic courses in the preparation for the superintendency. From the 1,207 respondents (11 no responses), superintendents were asked to rate sixteen courses typically taught in academic leadership preparation courses regarding the importance and relevance of each for the work done in the superintendency. The rating choices were *Extremely important, Moderately important, Unimportant, Courses were unavailable,* and *Chose not to take course(s)in this area.* Respondents were able to rate any number of courses as *Extremely important* and not required to rank the courses in priority order.

Figure 6.1 illustrates that school law was viewed as the most important course (73.24%), and school finance was the second in importance (66.75%), both rated as *Extremely important.* Moreover, the remaining fourteen courses were viewed as *Extremely important* by less than half of the participating superintendents, whereas 26.32% of the respondents rated research related courses as *Unimportant*—the highest in unimportance in superintendent preparation.

Comparing the *AASA 2020* results to the previous the *American School Superintendent: 2010 Decennial Study* indicates that the top choices of courses remained consistent with school law and school finance being the top two choices and school public relations and human resource management as the third and fifth choices, respectively.

Evaluation of Academic Preparation Programs

The second part of this analysis explores the overall evaluation of the academic preparation program by superintendents. From the 1,210 (8 no responses), superintendents were asked to indicate which category (*Excellent, Good, Average, and Inadequate*) describes an overall evaluation of their academic program in preparation for the superintendency. More than half of the respondents (54.88%) indicated their academic preparation was *Good* and 24.05% indicated it was *Excellent.*

The results were almost identical to 78.7% of respondents in the *American School Superintendent: 2010 Decennial Study,* who stated their preparation was either *Excellent* or *Good.*

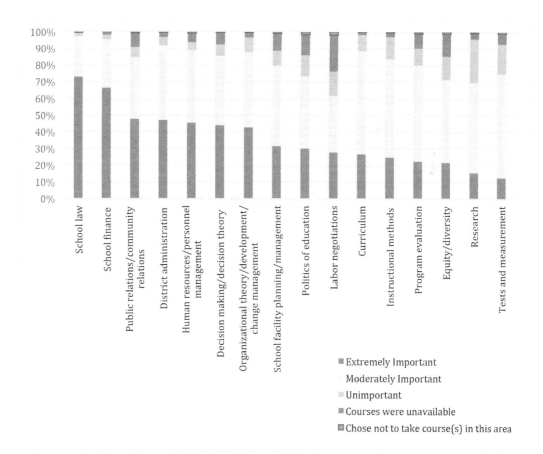

Figure 6.1. Distributions of Academic Courses Ranked by Importance to Superintendent Preparation Programs.

When considering the intersection of demographics and the *AASA 2020* study district demographics such as size, race, special populations, and ethnicity indicated negligible differences in the superintendents' overall program preparation evaluation. In addition, superintendent characteristics such as gender, race, or ethnicity revealed no rating differences. Furthermore, regardless of their highest degree, the majority of superintendents rated their program as *Good* in academic preparation for the superintendency with the exception of superintendents whose highest degree was an MBA (31.25%).

Credibility of Professors

The third part of this analysis explores superintendents' perceptions about the credibility of their professors in their educational administration/leadership courses. From the 1,211 (7 no responses), superintendents were asked to rate the credibility of the professors in their educational administration/leadership courses. Choices of evaluation ratings were *Excellent, Good, Average, and Inadequate.* The majority (80.09%) of superintendents indicated their professors in their superintendent preparation programs were *Good* or *Excellent.* The results of the *AASA 2020* study were almost exactly the same as the results from the *American School Superintendent: 2010 Decennial Study:* (81.1%). Interestingly, superintendent characteristics such as gender, race, or ethnicity revealed yielded no significant differences.

EXECUTIVE COACHING

This section examines (1) executive coaching prior to assuming the superintendency; (2) executive coaching for sitting superintendents; (3) district provisions and allocations for executive coaching; and (4) the importance of the relationship with executive coaches.

Prior to Assuming the Superintendency

The first part of this analysis explores whether superintendents had an executive coach prior to assuming the superintendency. From the 1,212 respondents (6 no responses), 90.18% indicated they did not have an executive coach prior to assuming the position; whereas 9.82% respondents indicated they had an executive coach before becoming a superintendent. When examining key demographic information, regardless of (1) district size; (2) superintendents' gender; (3) superintendents' racial/ethnic background; (4) superintendents' years of experience in current school district and in general; (5) superintendents' highest degree; and (6) superintendents' field of study in their highest degree, most of the superintendents did not have an executive coach before becoming superintendent.

Interesting to note was that superintendents whose field was in early childhood, elementary, middle, or secondary teaching showed the highest rate (28.57%) to experience executive coaching prior to assuming the superintendency, whereas superintendents whose field was curriculum and instruction had the lowest rate (3.57%) of receiving executive coaching prior to assuming the superintendency. It is worthy to mention that all superintendents whose field was in the realm of legal studies (N=4) indicated that they did not receive executive coaching before becoming a superintendent.

For Current Superintendents

The second part of this analysis examines executive coaching of superintendents once in the position. From the pool of 1,212 respondents (6 no responses), 69% indicated they did not receive executive coaching during their tenure as superintendent; whereas, 31% of the respondents indicated they had executive coaching during tenure as superintendent. Irrespective of their years of experience in their current school districts, a majority of the participating superintendents have not received executive coaching during their tenure as superintendent, regardless of their highest degree and field of study in their highest degree. Conversely, a majority of the participating superintendents who believed they are *Not at all effective* on district finance and budgeting received executive coaching during their tenure as superintendent.

When examining size, superintendents working in school districts with less than fifty thousand students were less likely to receive executive coaching during their tenure as superintendent. Relative to gender, a higher percent of female superintendents (32.29%) received executive coaching during their superintendency than male superintendents (30.64%). Moreover, the superintendents who chose *other* as their gender (N=2) received executive coaching during their superintendency.

Superintendents whose field is in early childhood/elementary/middle/secondary teaching were less likely (14.29%) to receive executive coaching during their tenure as superintendent, whereas superintendents whose field is special education were more likely (46.15%) to receive executive coaching during their tenure as superintendent. Noteworthy, participating superintendents' rate of receiving executive coaching during their tenure is higher (31%) than their rate of having an executive coach before becoming a superintendent (9.82%). The data were clear that even if superintendents received executive coaching, the experience was ranked as *Ineffective*.

District Provisions

The third part of this analysis examines whether school districts provide or pay for executive coaching for superintendents. From the 1,158 respondents (60 no responses), 17% of the participating districts provide or pay for executive coaching for their superintendents. Regardless of superintendents' race, the majority of the superintendents whose districts provide or pay for executive coaching was male (69.93%), except for Hispanic female superintendents (55.56%) whose districts provide or pay for executive coaching. Interestingly, none of the superintendents who choose not to indicate their gender (N=2) were provided with paid executive coaching by their districts, while all the superintendents who stated their gender as "other" were provided an executive coach, and these services were paid for by their districts.

Relationships

The fourth part of this analysis examines superintendents' perceptions about the importance of relationships with executive coaches to make career-related decisions. From the 837 respondents (390 no responses), the majority of superintendents stated that their relationship with their executive coach related to helping them make career decisions was *Unimportant.* The majority of male superintendents (62.34%) stated that their relationship with their executive coach in helping them make career decisions was *Unimportant*, while only 44.39% of female superintendents stated the same. Regardless of length of service as a superintendent, a majority of superintendents stated that their relationship with their executive coach in helping them make career decisions was *Unimportant*.

PROFESSIONAL LEARNING

This section examines professional learning related to the (1) quality of programs offered outside of the formal university setting; (2) organizations (providers) that sponsored professional learning programs since becoming a superintendent; (3) topics and focus of future professional learning opportunities; (4) types and preferences of readings superintendents prefer; and (5) skill areas superintendents want to improve.

Quality of Programs Offered Outside of Universities

The first part of this analysis examines superintendents' perceptions about the quality of professional learning programs offered outside of the formal university setting. From the 1,208 respondents (9 no responses), 38.43% indicated that the professional learning programs pertinent to their position provided outside of universities were *Excellent*; 48.51% indicated they were *Good*; 12.23% indicated they were *Average*; and 1.16% they were *Inadequate*. According to the data based on superintendents' gender and racial/ethnic group, most superintendents (48.54% for gender, and 48.83% for racial/ethnic group) stated the professional learning programs pertinent to their position provided outside of universities were *Good*. The next data set examines gender and race and the ratings about the quality of professional learning programs offered outside of the formal university setting as illustrated in figure 6.2.

Professional Learning Programs Taken Since Becoming a Superintendent

The second part of this analysis examines the professional learning programs sponsored by organizations that the superintendents completed since assuming the position. Participants were asked to select all the programs they had completed. From the 1,200 respondents (18 no responses) and a total of 3,911 responses, 91.75% indicated that they completed professional

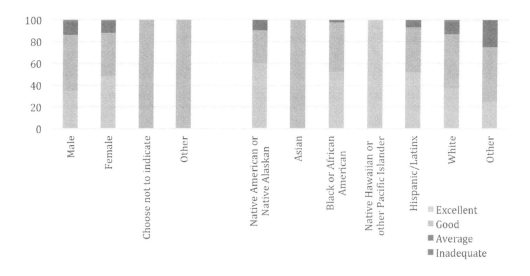

Figure 6.2.   Superintendents' Perceptions about the Quality of Professional Learning Programs Provided Outside Universities (by Gender and Race and Ethnicity)

learning programs sponsored by their state superintendent/administrator associations as illustrated in figure 6.3.

The data indicated that regardless of superintendents' gender and racial/ethnic background, a majority of superintendents attended professional learning programs offered by the state superintendent associations. Moreover, the data also showed that superintendents preferred to attend professional learning programs sponsored by their state superintendent/administrator association over any other organizations regardless of their race and gender. There was one exception in that 75.61% of black/African American superintendents preferred to attend professional learning programs offered by the American Association of School Administrators (AASA) while 70.73% of the respondents as a whole preferred programs offered by the state superintendent associations.

Data from the *AASA 2020* study mirrors data from the *American School Superintendent: 2010 Decennial Study* in that the most attended programs were offered by the state superintendent associations, followed by those offered by other associations and/or groups and the AASA.

Topics and Focus of Future Professional Learning Opportunities

The third part of this analysis examines the topics and focus of the next professional learning opportunities that superintendents would seek for themselves. From the 1,209 respondents (9 no responses), most superintendents (40.69%) indicated that they would seek continuous improvement [system-wide] as a future professional learning topic as illustrated in figure 6.4.

Superintendents sought to attend professional learning opportunities mostly related to continuous improvement regardless of the percentage of (1) racial and/or ethnic background of students; (2) students eligible for free/reduced lunch; (3) students enrolled as English Language Learners; (4) students qualified for special education with the exception of superintendents who worked in districts where 26% to 50% of the students qualified for special education. Responses came from a significant population of superintendents across multiple states. Data indicated that 13.38% of these superintendents who worked in districts with 6% or more

Figure 6.3. **Organizations That Superintendents Have Joined to Fulfill Professional Learning Needs.**

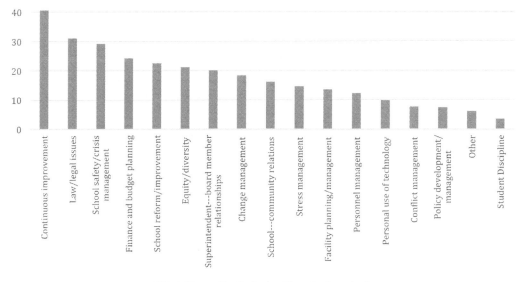

■ Topic/Focus of the Professional Learning Opportunity

Figure 6.4.   Topics and Focus of Future Professional Learning.

immigrant/refugee students were more likely to seek professional learning about equity/diversity.

Given shifts in student demographics and the rise in K–12 students of "unauthorized immigrants," it makes sense for superintendents to want to seek professional learning to support system-wide efforts to address such issues as poverty, deportation, and equity to be able to engage in "difficult conversations about difference and change, and to finding ways to capture the opportunities that emerge from a changing student population to improve teaching and learning" (Tamer, 2014, para 14). Analysis by district size illustrates that 40.85% of superintendents who work in the smallest school districts (fewer than 300 students) reported they would seek to participate in professional learning on finance and budget planning, and most of the superintendents who worked in a district with 50,000–99,000 students wanted to participate in professional learning on school safety/crisis management and equity/diversity.

The findings related to district size make sense given that smaller school districts often have fewer central office leaders. Superintendents in small districts must assume leadership across multiple areas such as budgeting, human resource administration, and special education. School safety issues seem to play a more prominent role in larger school districts (n=50,000–99,000). Superintendents in large districts indicated that safety and crisis management is a focus for professional learning. School safety, crisis preparedness, and threat assessment are areas that cannot be left to chance. Crisis management is more than response. It is comprised of prevention and intervention, response, and communication (Lalonde and Roux-Dufort, 2013; Liou, 2015).

Preparation and experience are the filters by which superintendents perceive their professional learning needs. As for years of experience, superintendents who spent one or less years in the superintendency will seek to attend professional learning opportunities related to finance and budget planning (42.75%); whereas superintendents with two or more years' experience will seek professional learning related to continuous improvement. Moreover, when examining the years of experience in their current district, superintendents (36.80%) with nine to twelve years of experience indicated school safety/crisis management and 43.40% of superintendents with thirteen or more years of experience indicated law/legal issues as the topic of their desired professional learning opportunities.

Also examined were the relationships between the areas that superintendents spend most of their time on and the topics of professional learning opportunities they will seek to attend. In terms of aligned topics, the majority of superintendents (50.63%) who spend most of their time on school safety/crisis management also seek to attend professional learning opportunities related to this area. Moreover, the majority of superintendents (80.77%) who spend most of their time on educational equity/diversity seek to attend the professional learning opportunity in the same area. Furthermore, many superintendents (44.59%) who spend most of their time on law/legal issues seek to attend the professional learning opportunity related to this area as well. There was no alignment in the remaining areas that superintendents spend most of their time with the topics of professional learning opportunities they want to attend.

There are, however, some striking relationships between superintendents' field of study of the highest education degree and the topical areas of the next professional learning opportunity they will seek. For example, 43.71% of the superintendents whose highest degree was in the field of educational administration/supervision sought to attend continuous improvement related to professional learning programs as their next focus. Moreover, 38% of the superintendents whose highest degrees were in the field of special education sought professional learning on school safety/crisis management. Furthermore, the professional learning opportunities about school safety/crisis management was the least chosen topic for superintendents holding any type of doctorate degree.

In the *American School Superintendent: 2010 Decennial Study,* superintendents were also asked to identify the potential continuing education topics that were relevant, and the three topics that were identified were law/legal issues, finance, and personnel management. By comparison, in the present study, the three topics identified were continuous improvement, law/legal issue, and school safety/crisis management.

Superintendent Reading Preferences

The fourth part of this analysis examines reading preferences of the superintendents. From the 1,197 responses (21 no responses), 72.68% stated they were more likely to read articles written with education practitioners in mind; 19.30% stated they were more likely to read articles written for leaders, not education-focused; and 8.02% stated they were more likely to read original research. When examining the superintendents' gender, racial/ethnic background, most of the superintendents were more likely to read articles written with school practitioners in mind, except those who indicated *other* for their gender or racial/ethnic background.

Although in the 2020 study superintendents were asked what type of research they were more likely to read, in the *American School Superintendent: 2010 Decennial Study,* superintendents were asked how often they read research relevant to the superintendent's position and the extent to which the research they read was beneficial. Most superintendents (approximately 92%) reported reading research *Frequently* or *Occasionally*, and the majority of superintendents (approximately 90%) found the research they read to be beneficial *Occasionally*.

Skill Areas Superintendents Want to Improve

The fifth part of this analysis examines the skill areas that superintendents want to improve. From the pool of 1,198 respondents (20 no responses), 29.97% stated they wanted to improve their skills in school reform/improvement; 28.97% wanted to improve in finance; and 26.13% wanted to improve in curriculum/instructional issues. The complexity of schools situates the superintendents as a key decision maker.

DECISION MAKING

This section examines superintendents' perceptions of identified influences on decision making and (1) previous professional experience, (2) district's administrative team, (3) fellow superintendents, (4) school board, (5) academic coursework, and (6) executive coach.

Previous Professional Experience

From the 1,205 respondents (13 no responses), previous professional experience was identified as having the strongest influence (59.75%) on superintendent decision making regardless of student demographics or superintendents' racial/ethnic background. While both males and females reported previous professional experience as having a strong influence on decision making, females reported greater influence (63.06%) than males (58.38%).

Superintendents of districts with 100,000 or more students reported a higher response (75%, N=3) of previous professional experience having an influence on their decision-making. Overall, a majority of the superintendents reported that previous professional experience exerted a strong influence on their decision making. Interestingly, a detailed analysis revealed that beginning superintendents with one year or less of experience gave a higher rating to previous experience effects on their decision making (72.66%). In contrast, previous professional experience appeared less influential the longer the superintendent served in the same district.

The connections between superintendent experience and decision-making influence is interesting to examine in relationship to superintendent turnover. Studies conducted in multiple states reveal interesting nuances in superintendent turnover (Grissom and Anderson, 2012; Grissom and Mitani, 2016; Hart, Schram-Possinger, and Hoyle, 2019). There are many reasons a superintendent might leave, such as more attractive job opportunities or poor relationships with a school board. Regardless, turnover is most common in urban and rural districts (Grissom and Anderson, 2012; Kamrath and Bruner, 2014).

Regardless of reason or size of district, turnover negatively impacts a district's performance as successful systemic reform takes five or more years (Grissom and Anderson, 2012). In light of these decision-making influences, high turnover implies that previous and multiple district experiences will have a greater effect on a superintendent's decision making than on superintendents who have a longer tenure in the same school district.

District Administrative Team

From the 1,204 respondents (14 no responses), the second highest-ranked influence on decision making was the district administrative team (46.84%). A slightly higher percentage of males (46.92%) than females (45.86%) reported the district administrative team greatly influenced their decision making.

Examining the results of the *Study of the American Superintendent: 2015 Mid-Decade Update*, superintendents in that study ranked fellow administrators along with board members as holding the greatest influence on decision making. In the *American School Superintendent: 2010 Decennial Study*, the influence of the administrative team was worded differently yet is comparable. Superintendents were asked if district administrators were valued as a major asset. The results in the 2010 study indicate that district administrators were seen as a valuable asset varying by the size of the district. In districts with 3,000–24,999 students, 85.2% reported the district administrative teams having a strong influence and those over 25,000 students were similar (86.2%). However, in districts below 300 students, the district administrative influence reported was considerably less (26.2%). As the authors of the 2010 study indicated, the little influence of the administrative team in small districts is likely because fewer district level administrators are on staff in the smallest districts.

Fellow Superintendents

From the 1,203 respondents (15 no responses), the third highest-ranked influence on superintendent decision making was fellow superintendents (36.41%), with males reporting a slightly higher ranking (37.83%) than females (33.12%). In the *American School Superintendent: 2010 Decennial Study*, 65.9% of the respondents reported fellow superintendents' influence as considerable or moderate (60.5%). Results of the *Study of the American Superintendent: 2015 Mid-Decade Update* indicated that fellow superintendents (peers) influenced their decision making very or moderately significantly regardless of the district size.

School Board

From the 1,208 respondents (10 no responses), 28.39% of the participating superintendents reported that the influence of the school board on their decision making is strong. A slightly higher percentage of female (30.38%) than male superintendents (27.68%) reported that the school board had a strong influence on decision making.

In the *American School Superintendent: 2010 Decennial Study,* a much stronger influence was noted as 69 % of superintendents reported school board influence as considerable. It was also noted in the 2010 study that superintendents in districts with less than 300 students were slightly less likely to say the school board had a considerable influence on them.

Academic Coursework

From the 1,202 respondents (16 no responses), second from the bottom of the list of decision-making influences was academic coursework (14.31%). However, a slightly higher percentage of males (14.74%) reported that academic coursework had strong influence on decision making versus female superintendents (12.78%).

Executive Coach

From the 1,157 respondents (61 no responses), the lowest ranking in this study was the influence of an executive coach. A majority (56.17%) of the superintendents reported that there was no influence of an executive coach on their decision making. However, as reported earlier in this chapter, only 31% of respondents had an executive coach in their position as superintendent. Table 6.1 summarizes superintendent rating of degree of influence on their decision making.

CONCLUSION

The analysis in this chapter describes superintendents' responses to questions regarding academic preparation for the position, executive coaching, professional learning, and influences on decision making. The superintendents' overall perception of their preparation program was *Good* or *Excellent*; moreover, the majority of superintendents indicated that their professors in their preparation programs were either *Good* or *Excellent.* The master's was the highest degree attained for over half of the superintendents. That degree, however, typically prepares candidates for the principalship, not district-level leadership.

It appears that executive coaching prior to or while in the superintendency is a relatively new practice that is in the process of defining itself and generating best practices. Given the overall aspects of executive coaching as presented in the robust research base in the business sector, the field of practice and its bridge to research is a critical area for further exploration. Findings indicate that very few superintendents had an executive coach before becoming a superintendent as well as during their superintendency. From the data, it is highly suggestive that districts may not support executive coaching considering the very small number of districts that provided or paid for executive coaching. Moreover, it is equally suggestive that the executive coach–superintendent relationship was viewed as *Unimportant* for executive coaches' influence on the vast majority of superintendents related to their decision making.

A vast majority of the superintendents believed that professional learning programs pertinent to their position provided outside of universities were *Good* or *Excellent*, and they preferred to attend professional learning programs in their state superintendent/administrator associations. Superintendents tended to read articles written with education practitioners in mind. The top three opportunities for future professional learning that superintendents desired to pursue focused on continuous improvement, law/legal issues, and school safety/crisis management. The highest-ranking areas that superintendents wanted to improve their skills included school reform/improvement, finance, and curriculum/instructional issues.

A superintendent's position requires decision making and is arguably a function that fundamentally impacts a district's direction, culture, and community perception. Superintendents rely predominantly on their previous professional experiences when making decisions, but this influence becomes less influential the longer the superintendents remain in the same district. The district administrative team was the second highest indicator in influence on superintendent decisions. In addition to previous experience and the district administrative team, fellow superintendents have a strong influence on decision making.

In conclusion, we recommend that future research focus on the specific content of preparation courses as well as professional learning more specifically on the duties, responsibilities, and the complexities of change associated with the position of the superintendent. From this

Table 6.1.   Ranked Categories Influencing Superintendent Decision Making

Categories	1 (strong influence)	5 (no influence)
Previous professional experience	59.75%	6.06%
District administrative team	46.84%	5.48%
Fellow superintendents	36.41%	5.24%
School board	28.39%	4.14%
Academic coursework	14.31%	5.66%
Executive coach	7.87%	56.27%

type of effort, perhaps the practice-to-research gap can be ameliorated through findings and recommendations to enhance effective superintendent competencies prior to and after obtaining the position.

As the expression goes, it is *lonely at the top*. To combat isolation in the context of school systems for superintendents, executive coaching, according to Harden and Stiles (2019), can potentially "accelerate the new superintendent's learning and . . . minimize missteps" because "each newcomer enters the position with a different set of skills and experiences, and each faces a different set of challenges. Coaching customizes the professional learning" (paras. 2–3). Executive coaching, superintendent networks, and other forms of professional learning are needed with topics that evolve at the pace in which schools, systems, and personnel change—constantly.

REFERENCES

Arar, K., and Avidov-Ungar, O. (2019). "Superintendents' Perception of Their Role and Their Professional Development in an Era of Changing Organizational Environment." *Leadership and Policy in Schools*, 1–15. https://doi.org/10.1080/15700763.2019.1585550.

Athanasopoulou, A., and Dopson, S. (2018). "A Systematic Review of Executive Coaching Outcomes: Is It the Journey or the Destination That Matters Most?" *The Leadership Quarterly* 29 (1), 70–88. https://doi.org/10.1016/j.leaqua.2017.11.004.

Björk, L. G., Browne-Ferrigno, T., and Kowalski, T. J. (2014). "The Superintendent and Educational Reform in the United States of America." *Leadership and Policy in Schools* 13 (4), 444–65. https://doi.org/10.1080/15700763.2014.945656.

Bredeson, P. V., Klar, H. W., and Johnsson, O. (2009). "Superintendents as Collaborative Learners in Communities of Practice: A Sociocultural Perspective on Professional Learning." *Journal of School Public Relations* 30 (2), 128–49. https://doi.org/10.3138/jspr.30.2.128.

Carnegie Project for the Educational Doctorate (CPED). (2009). *Working Principles for the Professional Practice Doctorate in Education.* College Park, MD: Author.

DiGirolamo, J. (2015). *Coaching for Professional Development.* Alexandria, VA: Society for Human Resource Management.

Ennis, S., and Otto, J. (2015). *The Executive Coaching Handbook: Principles and Guidelines for a Successful Coaching Partnership* (6th ed.). Retrieved from. http://www.executivecoachingforum.com.

Grant, A. M. (2014). "The Efficacy of Executive Coaching in Times of Organisational Change." *Journal of Change Management* 14 (2), 258–80. http://dx.doi.org/10.1080/14697017.2013.805159.

Grissom, J. A., and Andersen, S. (2012). "Why Superintendents Turn Over?" *American Educational Research Journal* 49 (6), 1146–80. https://doi.org/10.3102/0002831212462622.

Grissom, J. A., and Mitani, H. (2016). "Salary, Performance, and Superintendent Turnover." *Educational Administration Quarterly* 52 (3), 351–91. https://doi.org/10.1177/0013161X15627677.

Hanover Research. (2014). *Research Brief–Continuing Education for Superintendents.* Washington, DC: Author.

Harden, D., and Stiles, D. (2019). *Coaching Rookie Superintendents To Find Success.* Spotlight: American Association of School Administrators. Retrieved from https://www.aasa.org/SchoolAdministratorArticle.aspx?id=20834.

Hart, W. H., Schramm-Possinger, M., and Hoyle, S. (2019). "Superintendent Longevity and Student Achievement in North Carolina Public Schools." *AASA Journal of Scholarship and Practice* 15 (4), 4–13. Retrieved from https://www.aasa.org/.

Hollingworth, L., Sullivan, A. M., Condon, C., Bhatt, M., and Brandt, W. C. (2012). "Data-Driven Decision-Making in Higher Education: One University's Process of Revamping the Superintendent Licensure Program." *Journal of Research on Leadership Education* 7 (1), 78–97. https://doi.org/10.1177/1942775112440632.

Honig, M. I., and Rainey, L. R. (2014). "Central Office Leadership in Principal Professional Learning Communities: The Practice Beneath the Policy." *Teachers College Record* 116 (4), 1–48. Retrieved from http://www.tcrecord.org.

Jones, R. J., Woods, S. A., and Guillaume, Y. R. F. (2016). "The Effectiveness of Workplace Coaching: A Meta-Analysis of Learning and Performance Outcomes from Coaching." *Journal of Occupational and Organizational Psychology* 89 (2), 249–77. https://doi.org/10.1111/joop.12119.

Kamrath, B., and Brunner, C. C. (2014). "Blind Spots: Small Rural Communities and High Turnover in the Superintendency." *Journal of School Leadership* 24 (3), 424–51. https://doi.org/10.1177/105268461402400302.

Kowalski, T. J. (2013). *The School Superintendent: Theory, Practice, and Cases* (3rd ed.). Thousand Oaks, CA: Sage

Kowalski, T. J., McCord, R. S., Petersen, G. J., Young, I. P., and Ellerson, N. M. (2011). *The American School Superintendent: 2010 Decennial Study.* Lanham, MD: Rowman & Littlefield Education.

Lalonde, C., and Roux-Dufort, C. (2013). "Challenges in Teaching Crisis Management: Connecting Theories, Skills, and Reflexivity." *Journal of Management Education* 37 (1), 21–50. https://doi.org/10.1177/1052562912456144.

Levine, A. (2005). *Educating School Leaders*. Princeton, NJ: The Woodrow Wilson National Fellowship Foundation.

Liou, Y. (2015). "School Crisis Management: A Model of Dynamic Responsiveness to Crisis Life Cycle." *Educational Administration Quarterly* 5 (2), 247–89. https://doi.org/10.1177/0013161X14532467.

Perry, J. A. (2013). "Carnegie Project on the Education Doctorate: The Education Doctorate—a Degree for Our Time." *Planning and Changing* 44 (3/4), 113–26. Retrieved from http://works.bepress.com/jillaperry/16/.

Petersen, G. J., Fusarelli, L. D., and Kowalski, T. J. (2008). "Novice Superintendent Perceptions of Preparation Adequacy and Problems of Practice." *Journal of Research on Leadership Education* 3 (2), 1–22. https://doi.org/10.1177%2F194277510800300204.

Shulman, L. S., Golde, C., Bueschel, A. D., and Garabedian, K. J. (2006). "Reclaiming Education's Doctorate: A Critique and a Proposal." *Educational Researcher* 35 (3), 25–32. https://doi.org/10.3102/0013189X035003025.

Spanneut, G., Tobin, J., and Ayers, S. (2011). "Identifying the Professional Development Needs of School Superintendents." *International Journal of Educational Leadership Preparation* 6 (3), 1–15. Retrieved from http://www.ncpeapublications.org

Tamer, M. (2014). "The Education of Immigrant Children." *Usable Knowledge*. Retrieved from https://www.gse.harvard.edu/news/uk/14/12/education-immigrant-children.

Tripses, J., Hunt, J. W., and Watkins, S. G. (2013). "Voices of Superintendents: Give Us Relevant and Challenging Preparation for a Tough Job." *AASA Journal of Scholarship and Practice* 10 (3), 3–14. Retrieved from https://www.aasa.org/jsp.aspx.

Zepeda, S. J. (2019a). *Professional Development: What Works* (3rd ed.). New York, NY: Routledge.

Zepeda, S. J. (2019b). "Job-Embedded Professional Learning: Federal Legislation and National Reports as Levers." In M. L. Derrington and J. Brandon and (Eds.). *Differentiated Teacher Evaluation and Professional Learning: Policies and Practices for Promoting Teacher Career Growth* (pp. 173–95). New York, NY: Palgrave Publishing.

Zepeda, S. J., Bengtson, E., and Parylo, O. (2012). "Examining the Planning and Management of Principal Succession." *Journal of Educational Administration* 50 (2), 136–58. https://doi.org/10.1108/09578231211210512

Zepeda, S. J., Jimenez, A., and Lanoue, P. D. (2015). "New Practices for a New Day: Principal Professional Development to Support Learning Cultures in Schools." *LEARNing Landscapes* 9 (1), 303–19. https://doi.org/10.36510/learnland.v9i1.759.

Chapter Seven

Community Relationships

Sonya Douglass Horsford, Meredith Mountford, and Jayson W. Richardson

Building meaningful and authentic community relationships is an important aspect of the American school superintendency—the nature of which varies from district to district and community to community. Historically, school buildings served not only as the places where children gathered daily to learn in multi-age settings, but also as town halls, churches, and centers of community life. Although our nation's public schools are still used for town or city events, over time, they have lost the centerpiece status they once held (Kirst and Wirt, 1997). Consequently, this meant fewer community members, particularly those who never had children, might only rarely, if ever, even enter a school building. Throughout the twenty-first century, it became increasingly clear that certain segments of the community were feeling alienated from their local school community (Grogan, 2000; Mountford and Wallace, 2019) with school desegregation efforts limiting the ability for parents representing "minority" communities to engage and contribute to school events, activities, and decision making.

Nevertheless, regardless of district size, student population, or geographic location, the question of whether or not students—no matter their racial, ethnic, or cultural background—are getting the educational resources and opportunities they need to become contributing members of society is fundamental to the superintendency. Whether leading school communities in areas experiencing economic decline, gentrification, suburbanization, immigration, ethnic succession, and/or resegregation, the larger racial and political realities facing superintendents have made issues of race and equity ones they must understand and be prepared to address (Horsford, Scott, and Anderson, 2019; Tillman and Scheurich, 2013; Wilson and Horsford, 2013).

Furthermore, technology has transformed the superintendency, resulting in increased attention to the need for a shared vision of technology use at the district level, the development of technology infrastructure, and an emphasis on professional development opportunities for educators and staff (Richardson and Sterrett, 2018). Relatedly, the expansion of social media use has introduced new considerations for superintendents, including how they might engage social media to promote the work of their districts and the extent to which they support the personal and professional use of social media by their teachers, principals, and staff members.

PURPOSES

This chapter shares the responses of superintendents surveyed for the AASA decennial study across three areas related to stakeholder and community involvement. First, we describe the need and desire for equity across stakeholders. We use the term "minority" to be consistent with the survey questions, recognizing that this term is problematic in that it is primarily used by dominant group members to describe non-white students, groups, and populations. Next, community involvement in specific areas or tasks such as strategic planning is discussed, as is the broader phenomenon community relations with a focus on historically underserved stakeholders. Finally, this chapter looks at how superintendents across the country use social media and how it has or has not made a difference in the way superintendents communicate with district stakeholders. In total, up to 1,218 superintendents responded to the survey. However, not all respondents answered each question. Therefore the number of respondents varies by question.

EQUITY

Equity remains an increasingly important and complex issue for the American school superintendent. Educational leadership research in particular has emphasized the importance of racial literacy and culturally relevant and responsive leadership practices in pursuit of educational equity and excellence for all students (Horsford, Grosland, and Gunn, 2011; Khalifa, Gooden, and Davis, 2016; Theoharis and Scanlan, 2015; Wilson and Horsford, 2013). Such work often begins with having the preparation and capacity to lead what are often sensitive and difficult conversations concerning race at the school and local community level. Given widening and deepening racial and economic inequality across the country, superintendents are confronted by a politics of race and equity that can challenge and even undermine their attempts to lead their districts effectively.

In the 2020 study of American school superintendents, ten questions focused on race and equity broadly with six of those questions asking about *conversations* and *discussions* about race or equity and one question exploring whether such conversations lead to meaningful change. There was one question about professional development around equity issues and two questions inquiring about the superintendent's relationship with their "minority community" and a general question about local community relations. It is important to note that in the decennial study, the modal superintendent was a married, white (91.38%) male with 2–8 years of experience as a superintendent. In addition, 54.85% of respondents to these questions were rural superintendents, compared to 20.7% representing suburban districts, 18.92% in small town districts, and only 5.48% leading urban districts.

When asked about the importance of leading conversations on race by geographic location, as shown in table 7.1, 40% of superintendents identified it as *Extremely important*, 49.46% selected *Very important,* and 10.54% indicated such conversations were *Not important*. Responses varied by district location, with urban (59.09%) and suburban (56.40%) superintendents indicating their extreme importance compared to small town (39.91%) and rural (31.92%) superintendents who found conversations about race to be less important when compared to their peers in other contexts. There was also notable variation in how superintendents responded to this question based on their own racial/ethnic identity or group affiliation as outlined below in table 7.2. Among black superintendents, 65.85% reported that leading conversations about race was *Extremely important* compared to 58.62% of Hispanic/Latinx respondents and 36.63% of white respondents. Thirty-five percent of Native American or

Table 7.1. Importance of Superintendent Leading Conversations Regarding Race in District and Community by Geographic Location

Level of importance		Urban	Suburban	Small town/ city	Rural	Total
Extremely important	n	39	141	91	211	482
	%	59.09%	56.40%	39.91%	31.92%	40.00%
Important	n	25	99	118	354	596
	%	37.88%	39.60%	51.75%	53.56%	49.46%
Not important	n	2	10	19	96	127
	%	3.03%	4.00%	8.33%	14.52%	10.54%
Total	**n**	**66**	**250**	**228**	**661**	**1205**
	%	**5.48%**	**20.75%**	**18.92%**	**54.85%**	**100.00%**

Native Alaskan, 100% of Native Hawaiian or other Pacific Islander, and 50% of Asian superintendents (representing only one respondent) agreed that leading such conversations was *Extremely important*.

In terms of their preparedness to lead conversations on race, superintendents who described their leadership as being *Very effective* or *Somewhat effective* on the academic performance of their students indicated higher levels of preparation than those who did not (comprising only 2.25% of respondents). Most notable here are the numbers of superintendents who were *not at all prepared* to lead conversations on race, which included 20.08% of superintendents who rate themselves *Very effective* on the academic performance of students, 16.85% who identify as *Somewhat effective*, and 37.04% of those who deem themselves *Not effective at all* on student academic performance (see table 7.3).

Superintendents were asked about the extent to which equity conversations in their districts led to meaningful change. As presented in table 7.4, among those who described themselves as *very effective* on community building, 71.17% reported such conversations did lead to meaningful change, compared to 63.41% of those *somewhat effective* on community building, and only 38.46% of those who characterized themselves as *not effective at all*. In fact, 61.54% of superintendents who identified as ineffective in community building indicated that conversations about equity in their district did not lead to meaningful change.

Overall, superintendents reported feeling *very supported* or *somewhat supported* when asked to describe their relationship with their local community, and more specifically, the largest "minority community" in their districts. One increasingly important issue related to equity and community relations that invites greater study and attention relates to meeting the educational needs of immigrant and refugee students and their families entering U.S. schools, districts, and communities for the first time (see table 7.5). When asked about the importance of leading conversations about race based on immigrant/refugee population, 100% of superintendents with immigrant/refugee populations between 26 to 50% reported that such conversations are *Extremely important*. Of those superintendents leading districts with majority immigrant/refugee students populations, 80% indicated such conversations were *extremely important* and 20% identified them as *important*, compared to the 127 superintendents leading districts with fewer than 15% of students who are immigrants/refugees who reported that such conversations about race are *not important*.

Table 7.2.   Importance of Superintendent Leading Conversations Regarding Race in District and Community by Racial/Ethnic Group

Level of importance		White	Black	Hispanic/ Latinx	Native American or Native Alaskan	Native Hawaiian or other Pacific Islander	Asian
Extremely important	n	423	27	17	7	2	1
	%	36.63%	65.85%	58.62%	35.00%	100.00%	50.00%
Important	n	552	14	11	11	0	1
	%	50.41%	34.15%	37.93%	55.00%	0%	50.00%
Not important	n	120	0	1	2	0	0
	%	10.96%	0%	3.45%	10.00%	0%	0%
Total	**n**	**1095**	**41**	**29**	**20**	**2**	**2**
	%	**91.48%**	**3.43%**	**2.42%**	**1.67%**	**0.17%**	**0.17%**

Table 7.3.   Level of Preparedness to Lead Conversations on Race Based on Perceived Effectiveness on the Academic Performance of Students

Level of preparedness		Very effective	Somewhat effective	Not effective	Total
Very prepared	n	118	137	3	257
	%	22.14%	21.37%	11.11%	21.45%
Sufficiently prepared	n	308	396	14	717
	%	57.79%	61.78%	51.85%	59.85%
Not prepared	n	107	108	10	224
	%	20.08%	16.85%	37.04%	18.70%
Total	**n**	**533**	**641**	**27**	**1,198**
	%	**44.49%**	**53.51%**	**2.25%**	**100.00%**

Table 7.4.   Extent to Which Equity Conversations in Districts Led to Meaningful Change According to Superintendent Level of Effectiveness on Community Building

Extent of meaningful change		Very effective	Somewhat effective	Not effective	Total
Yes	n	395	279	5	679
	%	71.17%	63.41%	38.46%	67.43%
No	n	160	161	8	328
	%	28.83%	36.59%	61.54%	32.57%
Total	**n**	**555**	**440**	**13**	**1,007**
	%	**100.00%**	**100.00%**	**100.00%**	**100.00%**

Table 7.5. Importance of Superintendent Leading Conversations Regarding Race in District and Community Based on Immigrant/Refugee Population

Level of importance		Less than/ equal to 5%	6 to 15%	15 to 25%	26 to 50%	51% or more
Extremely important	n	369	66	21	10	4
	%	35.96%	55.46%	67.74%	100.00%	80.00%
Important	n	541	42	10	0	1
	%	52.73%	35.29%	32.26%	0%	20.00%
Not important	n	116	11	0	0	0
	%	11.31%	9.24%	0%	0%	0%
Total	**n**	**1,026**	**119**	**31**	**10**	**5**
	%	**86.36%**	**10.02%**	**2.61%**	**0.84%**	**0.42%**

In 2020, the superintendents' understanding of and appreciation for local community histories of social and educational inequality, coupled with an awareness and anticipation of how larger demographic, economic, and political trends shape and will continue to shape their districts, are foundational to their ability to lead for equity and excellence. As school communities continue to grapple with how best to handle racial and cultural conflict, sex and gender discrimination, and the treatment and protection of their most vulnerable students, superintendents who demonstrate leadership on issues of equity can have a positive and profound impact on school and community relations. With school districts serving as an important part of local communities and their civic infrastructure, equitable leadership remains an important priority for the American school superintendent.

COMMUNITY RELATIONS

Murphy (1991) and Brunner (2001) suggested minorities tended to feel unwelcomed in schools. Those who had been students there and were now adults living in the town reported negative feelings associated with school and expressed little desire to ever return, even if their children were currently attending the same school. This phenomenon remained consistent over time and district type, whether it was a rural, urban, suburban, or inner-city school district (Hess and Leal, 2001). The lack of the minority community members' involvement in school-related activities created a new responsibility for superintendents if they wanted input from all district stakeholders into important educational decisions, including mission and vision. Without the minority communities' voice, strategic initiatives would likely fail.

Six survey questions asked superintendents how they worked with district stakeholders and, more precisely, how they reached out to typically unrepresented stakeholders. It is important to keep in mind that while this may not seem like much of a challenge, the demographics of the superintendency and school boards has remained primarily white men since the position's inception.

One of the main functions of the superintendency is to serve as a human hub (Mountford, 2008) for the community, not unlike the school buildings as facilities hub. Regarding the level of support from their local community, almost all superintendents, 95%, reported feeling either *Very supported* (64.%) or *Somewhat supported* (31%) by their local community. However, when superintendents were asked about their relationship with the largest "minority" community, only 83% of superintendents reported feeling very or somewhat supported. This difference in the level of support superintendents reported feeling could very well be related to the difference in the types of concerns of the "minority" and "majority" communities.

When superintendents were asked if the "minority" community had concerns that were different from the concerns of the "majority" community, superintendents were almost evenly divided. The data suggest that 51% of respondents believed the "minority" community had concerns that were different from the majority community's concerns. Conversely, 49% did not think differences in concerns existed across the two groups. With only one notable exception, an almost even split persisted for this question regardless of demographics or school size. However, urban superintendents (70%) reported the "minority" and "majority" community were more likely to express divergent concerns (see figure 7.1).

Another clear disparity in responses had to do with the specific issues' superintendents reported as expressed by the "majority" or "minority" community. Figure 7.1 shows the level of concern for specific issues by "minority" and "majority" community members as perceived by the superintendents surveyed. It should come as no surprise the results show the primary areas of concern for "minority" community members were very different from those of the "majority" community members. Policy development and student discipline were of greatest concern for the "majority" community, whereas diversity and education equity were of greatest concern to the "minority" community.

Figure 7.2 shows the frequency superintendents reported engaging with parents and citizens for strategic planning or in advisory capacities. Somewhat surprisingly, over 83% of superintendents reported engaging with community either monthly (40.77%) or less than monthly (42.86%). It is somewhat disconcerting to learn that over 83% of superintendents reported engaging with parents and citizens a maximum twelve times a year and likely less while planning or for advisory purposes. One would expect superintendents to make greater

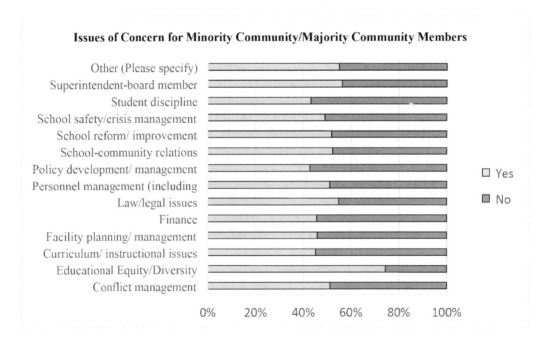

Figure 7.1.   Minority/Majority Concerns by Issue.

use of something that can increase buy-in to district objectives and loyalty in general (Grogan, 2000).

The lack of engagement suggests a disconnect with the constituents during important district planning purposes and decision making. However, this is one of the primary roles of the school board, which typically meet once a month. It is unclear if superintendents were considering the time they spend engaged with their board members at monthly board meetings or whether this was some other time with other constituents when they responded to this question. Roughly 80% of superintendents reported actively reaching out to "minority" communities when they are forming planning or advisory committees.

Regarding the level of involvement from the local community in activities such as, but not limited to, service clubs, committees, or fund drives, almost all superintendents reported some level of community involvement. Slightly over half (50.33%) of the superintendents surveyed reported the local community as being *Somewhat involved* in activities. Slightly less than half (45.42%) reported their local community as being *Very involved*. It appears that the local community is heavily involved in some of the activities of the school district but not necessarily involved in a planning or an advisory capacity for district initiatives.

Table 7.6 suggests that the functions/activities of local community members, including parents, tend to be more involved by geographic type. Overwhelmingly and regardless of district type, superintendents reported that over 70% of community members were involved in developing and setting a vision for the district and long-term strategic planning with the exception of small town and rural schools showing slightly less than 70% participation in long-term strategic planning. Other functions the community is commonly involved in, independent of district geographic type, were fundraising (67.96%) and facility planning (60.02%).

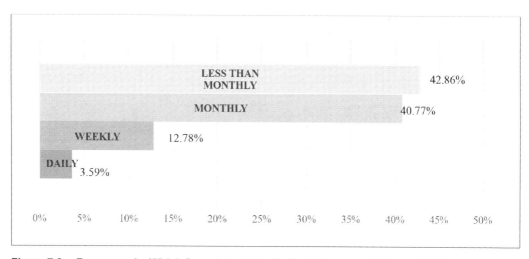

Figure 7.2.   Frequency by Which Superintendents Actively Engage with Parents/Citizens.

Table 7.6. Functions Community Stakeholders (Including Parents) Are Commonly Involved In, by District Geographic Location

District type		Urban	Suburban	Small town/city	Rural	Total
Constructing district or school visions	n	49	186	162	439	836
	%	4.14%	15.72%	13.69%	37.11%	70.67%
Curriculum revisions (e.g., adopting/revamping sex education)	n	18	84	60	155	317
	%	1.52%	7.10%	5.07%	13.10%	26.80%
Equity	n	28	103	58	142	331
	%	2.37%	8.71%	4.90%	12.00%	27.98%
Facility planning	n	37	155	153	365	710
	%	3.13%	13.10%	12.93%	30.85%	60.02%
Fiscal planning/management	n	20	71	73	152	316
	%	1.69%	6.00%	6.17%	12.85%	26.71%
Fundraising	n	43	170	150	441	804
	%	3.63%	14.37%	12.68%	37.28%	67.96%
Long-range or strategic planning	n	46	199	155	390	790
	%	3.89%	16.82%	13.10%	32.97%	66.78%

Program evaluation	n	12	60	47	173	292
	%	1.01%	5.07%	3.97%	14.62%	24.68%
Recommending policy and rules for co-curricular and extracurricular activities	n	20	50	60	197	327
	%	1.69%	4.23%	5.07%	16.65%	27.64%
Recommending policy and rules for student conduct/discipline	n	21	68	49	185	323
	%	1.78%	5.75%	4.14%	15.64%	27.30%
School attendance boundaries	n	25	86	36	62	209
	%	2.11%	7.27%	3.04%	5.24%	17.67%
Student transportation	n	10	36	18	79	143
	%	0.85%	3.04%	1.52%	6.68%	12.09%
Other	n	2	5	3	25	35
	%	0.17%	0.42%	0.25%	2.11%	2.96%
Total	n	**63**	**250**	**222**	**648**	**1,183**
	%	**5.33%**	**21.13%**	**18.77%**	**54.78%**	**100.00%**

SOCIAL MEDIA AND TECHNOLOGY

The 2020 AASA decennial study on the American superintendent included six questions that focused on the intersection of district leadership and digital technology. Various studies have been conducted on this specific population about this topic and each indicated that technology is changing the role of the American superintendent. For example, Richardson and Sterrett (2018) conducted a comparative study of district technology leadership from 2001 to 2014 and found that over this time period, superintendents matured in how they (a) used digital technology to foster a broad shared vision of technology use in the district; (b) focused on continual improvements to the infrastructure of the district; (c) embraced modern communication tools; (d) focused on individualized professional development for all staff members; and (e) embraced ambiguity.

McLeod, Richardson, and Sauers (2015) asked technology savvy superintendents what advice they might give to their peers. These district leaders suggested that superintendents must budget for technology and innovation, must serve as instructional leadership themselves around technology, must model professional learning about and through technology, must foster a professional learning network for technology, and must engage in personal risk-taking around the intersection of technology, learning, and leading. As such, including new questions to the decennial study around technology and district leadership is timely and relevant.

Using social media to promote the work of school districts seemed to be impacted by the number of years of experience as a superintendent. As detailed in table 7.7, superintendents with 2–4 years of experience seemed to be the heaviest users of all social media platforms where 36.6% of superintendents in this experience level used some form of social media to

Table 7.7. Using Social Media to Promote the Work of the District by Years of Experience as a Superintendent

Platform		1 or less years	2–4 years	5–8 years	9–12 years	13+ years	Total
Facebook	n	116	254	192	64	59	685
	%	11.96%	26.19%	19.79%	6.60%	6.08%	70.62%
Twitter	n	117	272	202	83	43	717
	%	12.06%	28.04%	20.82%	8.56%	4.43%	73.92%
Instagram	n	39	65	60	17	16	197
	%	4.02%	6.70%	6.19%	1.75%	1.65%	20.31%
Snapchat	n	4	10	12	2	3	31
	%	0.41%	1.03%	1.24%	0.21%	0.31%	3.20%
LinkedIn	n	48	83	80	34	15	260
	%	4.95%	8.56%	8.25%	3.51%	1.55%	26.80%
Blogs	n	29	52	39	19	11	150
	%	2.99%	5.36%	4.02%	1.96%	1.13%	15.46%
Podcasts	n	2	17	11	4	2	36
	%	0.21%	1.75%	1.13%	0.41%	0.21%	3.71%
Total	**n**	**161**	**355**	**272**	**105**	**77**	**970**
	%	**16.60%**	**36.60%**	**28.04%**	**10.82%**	**7.94%**	**100.00%**

promote the school district. Of interest, superintendents with a year or less of experience and experienced superintendents with more than nine years of service tended to have about the same levels of social media use (16.6% compared to 18.76%).

Superintendents were asked how effective they felt they were on various measures of social media use. Analyzing those data by superintendents use of any form of social media, we uncovered a few interesting findings. First, as detailed in table 7.8, very few superintendents reported being *Ineffective* on any measure as it related to using social media. Second, superintendents who used any form of social media tended to rate themselves as being *Very effective* around issues of school climate (64.21%) and perceptions of the district (68.35%).

When superintendents were asked if they had a person assigned to monitor the social media activities regarding the school district, 66.42% of respondents reported that they did. Only 17.56% of the superintendents with student populations greater than five thousand reported that a staff member actively monitored social media regarding their districts. This practice declines as the district gets larger. Figure 7.3 details the findings about having a dedicated person to monitor social media by urbanicity. As shown in table 7.9, districts with increased levels of diverse needs (i.e., racial/ethnic diversity, free/reduced lunch, qualified for special education, immigrants/refugees, English language learners, homelessness) tended to have a staff member assigned to monitor social media.

About 76% of superintendents encouraged the community to use social media to engage with the school district. When looking at these data across diverse needs (i.e., racial/ethnic diversity, free/reduced lunch, qualified for special education, immigrants/refugees, English language learners, homelessness), we did not see many differences when participants were asked about social media and community engagement.

Superintendents were asked if their school district encouraged principals and teachers to maintain social media accounts as way to communicate with parents and students. The responses indicate that 76.2% of urban districts confirmed this practice, in contrast to 77.5% of suburban districts, 70.2% of small-town districts, and 60.9% of rural districts. Figure 7.4

Table 7.8. Degree of Effectiveness Compared to Use of Any Form of Social Media

Effective on		Very effective	Somewhat effective	Not at all effective	Total
Student equity issues	n	501	482	11	989
	%	50.66%	48.74%	1.11%	100.00%
School climate	n	635	353	6	989
	%	64.21%	35.69%	0.61%	100.00%
Diversity issues	n	333	627	27	987
	%	33.74%	63.53%	2.74%	100.00%
Perception of district	n	678	307	10	992
	%	68.35%	30.95%	1.01%	100.00%
Academic performance	n	443	524	22	988
	%	44.84%	53.04%	2.23%	100.00%
Social-emotional learning	n	291	663	34	988
	%	29.45%	67.11%	3.44%	100.00%
Community building	n	551	428	12	990
	%	55.66%	43.23%	1.21%	100.00%

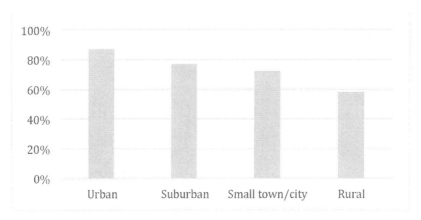

Figure 7.3.   Percentage of Districts That Monitor Social Media.

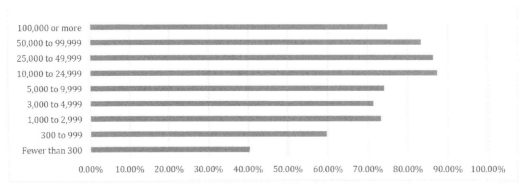

Figure 7.4.   Percentage of School Districts That Encourage Faculty Member Use of Social Media (by Size of Student Body)

shows that districts with larger student populations tended to encourage principals and teachers to maintain social media accounts.

As detailed in table 7.10, although rural superintendents were less likely to encourage principals and teachers to maintain social media accounts, they were more likely to post, respond, and maintain a social media presence themselves (54.2%), compared to superintendents in other locations. Nearly seven out of ten (68%) of the superintendents in the study indicated that social media was very helpful or moderately helpful to the day-to-day work of the district, whereas 4% of superintendents felt that social media was very disruptive.

SUMMARY

This chapter shared findings from the 2020 Decennial Study regarding the superintendents' self-reported interactions with community members with regard to both minority and majority factions and the specific projects they participate in, specific issues of concern, and their use of social media to enhance multiple-way communication with community member and other stakeholders. In 2020, a superintendent's understanding of and appreciation for local community histories of social and educational inequality, coupled with an awareness and

Table 7.9. Percentage of School Districts with a Staff Person Charged to Monitor Social Media, by Demographic Variable

Demographic variable	5% of less	6–15%	16–25%	26–50%	51% or more
Racial/ethnic diversity	56.62%	63.98%	72.46%	76.04%	76.37%
Free/reduced lunch	73.91%	66.67%	64.96%	65.07%	68.04%
Qualified for special needs	64.71%	69.88%	63.44%	52.54%	80.00%
Immigrants/refugees	63.96%	77.97%	86.21%	80.00%	100.00%
English language learners	61.17%	70.75%	77.36%	91.80%	66.67%
Homelessness	65.67%	65.57%	84.62%	71.43%	100.00%

Table 7.10. Level of Social Media Use of Superintendents, by Location

Level of social media use		Urban	Suburban	Small town/city	Rural
Post or respond to something on social media every day	n	19	61	38	110
	%	31.67%	25.10%	17.12%	17.71%
Post or respond to something on social media a few times a week	n	14	94	89	218
	%	23.33%	38.68%	40.09%	35.10%
Post or respond to something on social media a few times a month	n	11	46	42	137
	%	18.33%	18.93%	18.92%	22.06%
Maintain social media accounts but rarely check them and rarely post or respond to anything on them	n	16	42	53	156
	%	26.67%	17.28%	23.87%	25.12%
Total	**n**	**60**	**243**	**222**	**621**
	%	**5.24%**	**21.20%**	**19.37%**	**54.19%**

anticipation of how larger demographic, economic, and political trends will continue to shape their districts. These topics are foundational to their ability to lead for equity and excellence.

As school communities continue to grapple with how best to handle racial and cultural conflict, sex and gender discrimination, and the treatment and protection of their most vulnerable students, superintendents who demonstrate leadership on issues of equity can have a positive and profound impact on school and community relations. With school districts serving as an important part of local communities and their civic infrastructure, equitable leadership remains an important priority for the America school superintendent.

REFERENCES

Brunner, C. C. (2001). *Power and Authentic Participatory Decision-Making in the Superintendency: Effects on Social Justice*. Paper presented at the annual meeting of the University Council for Educational Administration, Cincinnati, OH.

Grogan, M. (2000). "Reconceptualizing the Superintendency." *Educational Administration Quarterly* 36 (1), 76–116.

Hess, F. M., and Leal, D. L. (2001). "Quality, Race, and the Urban Education Marketplace." *Urban Affairs Review* 37 (2), 249–66.

Horsford, S. D., Grosland, T., and Gunn, K. M. (2011). "Pedagogy of the Personal and Professional: Toward a Framework for Culturally Relevant Leadership." *Journal of School Leadership* 21 (4), 582–606.

Horsford, S. D., Scott, J., and Anderson, G. (2019). *The Politics of Education Policy in an Era of Inequality: Possibilities for Democratic Schooling.* New York: Routledge.

Khalifa, M. A., Gooden, M. A., and Davis, J. E. (2016). "Culturally Responsive School Leadership: A Synthesis of the Literature. *Review of Educational Research* 86 (4), 1272–1311.

Kirst, M. W., and Wirt, M. F., (1997). *The Political Dynamics of American Education* (4th ed). Berkeley, CA: McCutchen.

McLeod, S., Richardson, J. W., and Sauers, N. J. (2015). "Leading Technology-Rich School Districts: Advice from Tech-Savvy Superintendents." *Journal of Research on Leadership Education* 10 (2), 104–26.

Mountford, M. (2008). "Historical and Current Tensions among School Board/Superintendent Teams: Symptom or Cause?" In T. Alsbury (Ed). *Relevancy and Revelation: The Future of School Board Governance.* Lanham, MA: Rowman & Littlefield Press.

Mountford, M., and Wallace, L. (2019). "R(E)volutionary Leadership: An Innovative Response to Rapid and Complex Change." In M. Mountford and L. Wallace (Eds*.) The Contemporary Superintendent: (R)Evolutionary Leadership in an Era of Reform.* (pp. 1–12) Information Age Press (IAP): Charlotte, NC. In M. Mountford and L. Wallace, *Research on the Superintendency and School Governance.* A three-book series published with Information Age Press, Charlotte, NC.

Murphy, J. (1991). *Restructuring Schools: Capturing and Assessing the Phenomena.* New York, NY: Teachers College Press.

Richardson, J. W., and Sterrett, W. L. (2018). "District Technology Leadership Then and Now: A Comparative Study of District Technology Leadership from 2001 to 2014." *Educational Administration Quarterly* 54 (4), 589–616.

Theoharis, G., and Scanlan, M. (Eds.) (2015). *Inclusive Leadership for Increasingly Diverse Schools.* New York, NY: Routledge.

Tillman, L. C., and Scheurich, J. J. (2013). *Handbook of Research on Leadership for Equity and Diversity.* New York, NY: Routledge.

Wilson, C. M., and Horsford, S. D. (Eds.). (2013). *Advancing Equity and Achievement in America's Diverse Schools: Inclusive Theories, Policies, and Practices.* New York, NY: Routledge.

Chapter Eight

Leading in Transition

Joshua P. Starr

"We can't keep up with the pace of change, let alone get ahead of it. At the same time, the stakes—financial, social, environmental, political—are rising. The hierarchical structures and organizational processes we have used for decades to run and improve our enterprises are no longer up to the task of winning in this faster-moving world."
—John Kotter, *Accelerate*, 2012

American society is in an economic and demographic transition. The economy has shifted into the information and technological age, demographics are less white, and social and political institutions are eroding and being challenged. As society goes, so, too, go its public schools. It follows, then, that the role of the superintendent has and must evolve to meet these new demands, challenges, and opportunities. As previous chapters have shown, results of the 2020 AASA decennial survey of the superintendency provide some indication of how the role is constructed and how well prepared superintendents might be to lead through times of transition. Superintendents must do more to build on the legacies and strengths of the position, with an eye toward a potential new set of knowledge, skills, and competencies for those who will lead our public school systems well into the future.

Schools operate within a social context. What gets taught, who gets taught, who teaches, how and where learning occurs, and the metrics for success change with the times. Whether it was the inclusion of girls in public schools, the decline of explicit religious education, or the forced desegregation of school districts, schools have always been subject to societal forces. Today, as the societal forces within our nation continue to evolve, so must our schools. Superintendents must lead that change, but what direction should they head, and what knowledge, skills, and vision must they have in order for our public schools to better serve a more diverse student population? What, in fact, is the problem our schools are trying to solve, and how should a superintendent exercise the kind of leadership that will seize the opportunity to lead the change that is necessary for children, communities, and society?

One problem leaders must grapple with today is how to enable and prepare all children to graduate with the knowledge and skills needed to embrace an increasingly complex world on their own terms. The underpinnings of the economy and political order are not as strong as they once were, with income inequality at an all-time high amid a fractured and polarized citizenry. The old promise that hard work would enable one to seize the opportunity of being an American, —while available for some throughout our history—has diminished considerably for most Americans.

PURPOSE

Transition means moving toward something new, but it also means loss. What knowledge and skills that were essential in 2010 or 2015 may not be as relevant in 2020 and 2025? How can superintendents, who typically rise through the leadership ranks building on their expertise, develop new capacities and knowledge that will enable them to lead a system into an unknown future? How can they quickly respond to new conditions and demands without causing chaos? And how can they move entrenched bureaucracies that hold on to the status quo for dear life? What needs to be "unlearned," or what should superintendents stop doing in order to help their school system through this period of transition? This chapter focuses on how today's superintendents could lead during periods of economic and societal transitions by helping to lead their communities through a change management strategy focused on academics, talent management, and culture, through an equity lens.

TRANSITIONS

It is all too common for policy makers, product developers, and elected officials to claim that the jobs of tomorrow haven't been invented yet, and that schools need to be radically overhauled to prepare our students for a world that will exist in the future. Superintendents are then charged by bureaucrats with doing *something* in response to this spurious claim. Frankly, we know that the economy is in a transition, but we don't yet know what it means, which can make it difficult for a superintendent to lead toward the unknown. We know there will be further automation in manufacturing and other sectors like banking and financial service. An increase in service jobs and technology has changed how, when, and where people work. There are more jobs in health care today than ever before and climate change has the potential to upend the economy and the labor market dramatically.

The change in demographics in America are obvious to nearly everyone. Two of the major forces at work are a large aging population of predominantly white people (baby boomers) and a large population of much more racially diverse young people (millennials and Generation Z). According to Cilluffo and Cohn (2019) from the Pew Research Center, some of the demographic trends include a significant increase in the Latinx population—which is now the largest non-white group in the United States, more unmarried parents and single parent households, increases in income inequality, and immigration. Schools have typically not handled these types of change well, not necessarily because of their own actions but because of societal pressure that manifests in policies that restrict the ability of schools to meet such needs.

Although there are roughly an equal number of registered Democrats, Republicans, and Independents, the partisan divides keep growing (Laloggia, 2019; Pew Research Center, 2017). At the local level, most political debates tend to be about bread-and-butter issues, although in some communities the national hyper-partisanship has a trickle-down effect. It's not yet clear how the next generation of parents, taxpayers, and employees will act when they start to have some political power. Will the polarization increase, or will they chart a new course? Regardless, a superintendent must attend to the current realities of national and local political discourse and the potential desired future.

Finally, superintendents must contend with changes to the social fabric of America. As explained in chapter 7, social media plays an ever-increasing role in the discourse of school systems and communities. Arguments, accusations, rumors, and false claims abound online, and they increase the pressure on school leaders to be aggressively public facing. And because people tend not to gather in community anymore, the polarizing rhetoric serves to divide when increased personal interaction could build bridges and relationships. The decline in two-parent households has direct implications for school systems, as does the increased economic stratification. Social justice issues, such as climate change, institutional racism, economic and educational inequities, and the rights of LGBTQ people loom larger than ever. Stakeholders expect superintendents to have answers that attend to the interests of everyone in the community.

LEADING DURING TRANSITION

What should superintendents do to lead amid these changes, and how do they continue to sail a steady ship while preparing their communities and schools for the unknown? The first issue public school system leaders must face is how their work has been defined for the last twenty years. Superintendents' efforts to transform systems have been squeezed by three distinct factors. First are the federally driven mandates for accountability that rely on annual standardized tests. The No Child Left Behind Act exposed the underbelly of inequities that have always existed in American public schools. Yet the rigidity of the solutions did not lead to the desired improvements in student achievement.

Narrow interpretations of federal law and subsequent spending requirements of Federal Title dollars, coupled with an aggressive marketplace, resulted in schools and districts buying new programs every few years, each holding the promise of rapid student achievement gains. Every year schools go through a school improvement planning process that may focus some efforts and move some metrics for a short period of time without sustaining or scaling lasting change. School leaders adopt data-based decision-making processes, undergo new professional development, or conduct school and classroom walk-throughs, all with mixed results. Every year school board members and local politicians decry the increase in expenditures that have not led to commensurate expected results, and the superintendent has to develop a new plan or strategy with the promise that this time it will be different.

A second factor that has narrowed the lane within which a superintendent leads has been the philanthropic community. Of course, not all districts receive foundation support. In fact, the Gates Foundation and others like it have invested in only a few districts, organizations, and states. Yet, although the typical district might not directly receive funds from philanthropy, the influence of philanthropy on the terms of the debate about education reform has created a current that many superintendents find themselves swimming against.

Philanthropic investments have sparked innovation, forced some needed changes, and started necessary conversations. But they've also influenced the media, policy makers, and the larger ecosystem of professional associations, advocacy groups, and think tanks. Philanthropists set the terms of the debate by funding studies on their investments, supporting ideologically aligned groups, and actively promoting certain solutions. Superintendents who strive to properly contextualize these initiatives and purported panaceas as promising but limited are accused of maintaining the status quo or resisting innovation. Sometimes they follow suit because it is too difficult not to, or they don't have any better ideas, or they are pushed out for a new "change agent" superintendent.

The third factor superintendents must contend with as they seek to make change is the growing for-profit education marketplace. Publishing houses, testing companies, and technology outfits have commandeered the realm of possibilities for innovation. As standards shifted from individual state standards to a common set of curricular content for mathematics and English Language Arts in forty-two states and back to Common Core–aligned state standards, publishing companies seized the opportunity to bring new products to bear. Testing companies had to change their tests along with the standards, enable the tests to be computer based, and developed new reporting systems. Various products from technology companies captured the imagination of educators, policy makers, and funders by promising increased efficiencies, insights, and personalization, while school districts had to increase their investments in times of restrictions on funding.

The question becomes one of whether superintendents are prepared to embrace the opportunities this next decade holds. Previous chapters have delineated the history of the superintendency, current work of the superintendency, demographic profiles of superintendents, professional preparation, how superintendents continue to learn, and how they engage with the community. The data make it clear that while the job is a difficult one, it can be full of joy, too.

CURRENT WORK

Although superintendents have always been expected to lead all aspects of school systems, their success is typically measured by operational effectiveness and political acuity. Superintendents are rarely fired for inadequate student achievement, but a major financial or operational snafu can sink them. So, too, can the inability to make the right political connections, either through relations with the board of education or the ability to align the support of other formal and informal community leaders. Superintendents aren't likely to have enough expertise in every area of a school system's operations and must therefore supervise by asking the right questions of their leadership team.

Depending on the size of the district, the superintendent's cabinet is often made up of leaders of teaching and learning, finance and operations, human resources, technology, community engagement, principal supervision, and equity. In smaller districts, the superintendent may be leading many of those areas while the leadership team is composed of principals and an assistant or deputy who serves as the number-two leader in the district. The superintendent typically must solve the most difficult and complex problems in each of the areas, as the easier ones are often handled further down the chain of leadership. How, then, should superintendents find the right balance between the breadth and scope of the job and their own expertise and knowledge?

The superintendent must be the standard bearer for excellence and equity. Superintendents can be stewards of the community's values and must work to ensure that those values embrace high academic standards for each and every student and the alignment of resources to ensure that all students are able to achieve those standards. As the data presented in chapters 5 and 7 show, superintendents aren't always prepared to lead conversations in the community about race and equity, nor are their boards of education. How can they fulfill their responsibility of communicating a clear vision to everyone within the system, including employees, families, and community?

As presented in chapter 5, because of political interference, "some districts experience a lack of cohesive vision, mission, and core values" (Hutchings and Brown, 2020). Every day the superintendent must push an agenda with non-negotiable stakes in the ground related to equity and excellence. Whether that is through public pronouncements, social media, in meetings with employees or community leaders, superintendents must relentlessly provide an aspirational vision for what public schools can be. Yet, superintendents report that only 7 percent of their time is dedicated to issues of diversity and equity. This must change.

FOCUSING ON THE MAIN THING

If superintendents are going to act as standard bearers for excellence and equity and spend time communicating their visions, they must be clear about how they will manage and supervise their teams. The supervision process requires a shift in how data are used to inform decision making. Too often school systems rely on lagging indicators to make decisions, generally results from standardized tests taken months before the results are published. Although these scores might provide some general indication of where the challenges are and what kinds of supports and investments should be made, it does not enable the kind of quick adjustments and interventions that might need to be made.

Superintendents must also be clear about their unit of change. The principal is an important factor in school improvement. Simply put, there are no great schools without great principals. Yet, central offices sometimes overlook or bypass the principal when implementing change efforts by going straight to teachers and simply informing the principals rather than involving them. If the unit of change for the superintendent and the administrative team is the principal, they must design a system of support and accountability focused on continuous improvement and innovation. Such a system rests on three areas: (1) academics, (2) talent, and (3) culture.

TEACHING, LEARNING, AND EQUITY

Academics are the lifeblood of a school system. Superintendents must organize around these essential questions: What are students expected to know and be able to do? How will students be taught in such a way as to enable them to learn the things they must know and be able to do?

The results of the 2020 survey suggest that although superintendents might be hired for their instructional leadership, they spend much less time on that than other areas. Assuming they can't just change their schedules to devote more time to teaching and learning (although some modifications can surely be managed), it is essential that they focus on academic standards, leading assessment data, curriculum, and resources.

Whether it's the Common Core State Standards, individual state standards, or standards from professional organizations (e.g., NCTM, NCTE), superintendents must ensure that what gets taught every day, to every student, reflects what they actually need to know in order to graduate ready for post-secondary education, world of work, and responsible socio-civic participation. Hence, superintendents need to establish a process whereby they regularly review the written and taught curriculum. There are policy decisions within this process, as the board of education needs to require that all students have access to standards-driven curriculum. Following these decisions, there are three review processes that superintendents should follow with their teams: student access, curriculum and materials, and student learning.

At the macro-level, student access to standards-based content and the supports necessary to make full use of the access are two of the most important considerations for superintendents. Do all students have the opportunity and support to learn content that will prepare them for life after secondary school, whatever path they choose? If not, why, and which students don't have the kind of access or support necessary to reach their full potential? Superintendents must review, with their teams, how each principal assigns students to courses and determine whether there are formal or informal barriers that keep certain students from a rich curriculum. Then the principal must be supported to change practices, if necessary, to align with district policy and the evidence about student learning.

Students who are given low-level tasks tend to achieve at low levels. While there is certainly a role for remediation and support for students who need help, it must be in service of them accessing learning and content based on a high standard. Superintendents must be diligent in reviewing data prior to the start of the school year—and throughout—that can shed light on a principal's strategy for leading in support of this goal. They must also insist that their team is regularly reviewing these data and helping the school act on it.

At the micro level, superintendents need an understanding of whether curriculum and supporting documents are standards-based and culturally responsive. Again, board policy is an important lever, as they should regularly review and adopt new and revised curriculum. Superintendents must also have a process for managing the education marketplace, as state procurement policies and the tractor beam of the status quo can lead to disincentives for innovation. Curriculum audits can be a useful tool for superintendents to develop an understanding of the current state of instruction in the district, but they serve only to show broad strengths and deficiencies. Further analysis of supporting materials and what and how students are actually being taught every day are also necessary.

Leading data on student learning must be gathered regularly for superintendents to engage in instructional leadership. Rather than rely on state standardized test scores to inform their change management strategy, superintendents need a process that ensures student work and teacher assignments are regularly reviewed by school-level personnel and the central office. The superintendent and central office should insist that processes for instructional leadership are designed and executed well, and in smaller districts superintendents are often an active participant in those processes. Review of teachers' assignments and student work are essential components of leading teaching and learning because task predicts performance. By regularly reviewing who gets taught what and whether those assignments are likely to help a student learn the necessary knowledge and skills, superintendents can align resources and supports to help those principals who need it.

TALENT MANAGEMENT

Human resources, or talent management, is a cornerstone of a superintendent's change management strategy. At least 80 percent of a school district's budget is made up of people, and they are the ones doing the work every day with students. No curriculum, program, or technology can take the place of a well-prepared, supported, and inspired professional educator. Managing change means managing and leading people. Unfortunately, as the results from the 2020 survey show, although superintendents spend a lot of time on personnel management, the bulk of that time is spent on reactively addressing personnel issues rather than proactively designing talent management systems. To focus on the latter, there are three important factors in talent management: recruiting and hiring teachers, teacher assignments to courses, and professional learning.

Given the rates of teacher attrition in some districts, it can be difficult to be selective about who gets hired to teach. However, there are some things superintendents can do to ensure that they are at least hiring people who share the values of the district. Additionally, there are steps that can be put in place to develop a talent pipeline, as well as to retain and develop great educators. Recruitment is twofold: getting the right talent to apply to the district is one element and placing them in the proper school is another.

The Human Resources department should work closely with school principals to determine the knowledge and skills of the candidate. Principals are the unit of change so they must have a significant say in who works in their school. One strategy superintendents can employ is to work to align preservice programs with district expectations, so that whomever is sent to the principal for potential hiring has a baseline level of knowledge and skills deemed important by the district. To do this, the superintendent must leverage relationships with local universities. It's not clear whether the 30 percent of their time spent on community relations reported in the survey is directly aligned to building these kinds of partnerships.

The hiring process can be a great opportunity to clarify the candidate's values, especially concerning issues of race and equity. Asking a simply question like "Why is there an achievement gap?" can expose a candidate's beliefs about children. If they say, "Some parents just don't value education," their beliefs about the root causes of underachievement are made clear and it would be questionable to bring them into a district. When trying to attract candidates of color to the district it's important to show, if possible, that they're not going to be the only educator of color in the school, and that they won't be expected to deal solely with discipline of the students who look like them.

LEVERAGING EQUITY

Who gets assigned to teach which course is the key educational equity lever for a superintendent to pull. About half of superintendents are very comfortable leading for equity, although they indicated they do not spend much time on it. By starting with a focus on which teachers are in front of which kids and why, a superintendent can focus an equity agenda on a practical, everyday aspect of school systems. Superintendents need to put a system in place whereby their team works with principals to ensure that talent is assigned according to task. This means, at a bare minimum, putting the most effective teachers with the most vulnerable students. While the principal must have authority to assign teachers within the building to different courses, the superintendent and administrative team must have clear guidance and board of education policy for doing so, and the results of assignments must be reviewed via multiple data sources to determine the influence.

It is subsequently necessary for there to be a data system that allows principals and system leaders to understand the effectiveness and skills of various teachers. Given the relationship between teacher effectiveness and student learning, there is likely no greater issue to organize around than how teachers get assigned to students. The superintendent will have to apply all of his or her political skills to put such a system in place, given the traditional opaqueness of such processes and the tendency to consider all teachers as equally skilled, despite the evidence to the contrary.

Finally, a comprehensive talent management system rests on the continued professional learning of everyone in the system, including support professionals, classroom teachers, other faculty, and building and system leaders. Only 24 percent of respondents noted that school reform and improvement was a topic for their future professional development, yet superintendents have to put in place systems for the continuous development and support of the people in the district in order to ensure they have the right skills to help the students. Accountability can then be reciprocal, as they should not be held accountable for that which they cannot do. The challenge for superintendents is to design such systems so that their team is supporting school principals in a coherent fashion. If the central office is not set up to act accordingly, the superintendent's change management strategy must account for system leaders learning new skills—such as coaching and collaboration—and establish new processes to ensure alignment.

CULTURE

The old business school axiom that "culture eats strategy for lunch," is both frustrating for superintendents and all too true. Too many incentives for system leaders are aligned to strategies and tactics. Federal law requires states to institute accountability systems through mandated strategic planning processes. Such processes are supported by approaches to data-based decision making, SMART goals, objectives, stretch goals, and so on. A representative group of stakeholders must be part of the process to give it some authenticity. Low-performing students, as measured by state-mandated standardized tests, are designated for additional supports through the use of Federal Title dollars and new programs or technologies. Rinse and repeat.

These processes may be necessary to comply with federal and state law, but they are in no way sufficient for a superintendent to effect real change within the system. What is needed is a culture of continuous improvement and learning that rests on student needs, employee capacity, and a community's vision for its schools. The superintendent is the only person who can lead that effort and it requires a focus on serving the people in the organization so that they can do their best work. The results from the 2020 survey indicated that continuous improvement was the area where superintendents are most interested in having more professional learning.

Culture is manifest in four important ways in school systems: (a) employees, (b) students, (c) families, and (d) community. Employees view the superintendent through a "say-do" ratio; do superintendents do what they say they're going to do? If a superintendent states classroom instruction as the most important issue, how much time is spent visiting schools and talking about instruction? A superintendent who says he or she wants collaboration yet acts in a top-down fashion will not have much credibility with employees. Rewards and recognition are another key part of culture building among employees. Who gets rewarded for what kind of behavior is known and seen by a vast number of employees. Whether employees are held accountable for questionable behaviors or poor performance are open secrets in school systems. These issues are at the heart of school system cultures and must be measured and attended to by superintendents.

Students play an important role in a school system's culture and can provide incredible sustenance to, or detract from, a superintendent's change management strategy. Data suggests that students get increasingly disengaged from school the older they get. Although this may not affect the performance of more affluent, white, "just add water" kids in "first do no harm schools," it can have serious consequences for more vulnerable students. Students need to know that they are loved, valued, safe, and will be supported to achieve high academic standards. These needs can be measured and supported, and adults need to learn how to do so and be held accountable for such metrics. Given the largely white female teaching population and a growing number of students of color, superintendents must attend to racial dynamics in such efforts as well. Students should be involved in decision making at the school and system level and be given opportunities to lead. When superintendents show they value students, it can improve a district's culture and be a model for other leaders.

Superintendents spend a lot of time on family and community engagement, as shown in chapter 7. All too often, engaging with families can be seen as one-way, in that a system leader spends time informing families about what is going in the schools and gathering some feedback. Formal bodies such as parent councils and PTAs/PTOs may meet with the superintendent on a regular basis. Sometimes these meetings focus on issues that the leadership is pushing, which can imply that such meetings serve as a political means for getting change through. School-level meetings often follow the same pattern. These efforts may be necessary, but they run the risk of perpetuating the disenfranchisement of families of color and more vulnerable families by not sufficiently attending to their schedules and needs. Whoever shows up controls the discourse, and if families of the most vulnerable students aren't able to attend the meetings, their needs may not be on the table. Superintendents have a responsibility to show the system that all voices matter and then find ways to involve more than the usual suspects in decision making. Superintendents must also show that they are willing to listen to families and build a culture of community collaboration; white leaders have the additional responsibility of becoming allies to communities of color. These kinds of relationships are important elements of a school systems culture.

Finally, a superintendent's engagement with the community signals the overall culture of the system. How the leader interacts with the board of education, other elected officials, and key community leaders is seen by families and employees as a key marker of how the district operates. If board members can dictate personnel decisions or micro-manage district operations, employees know that while they may have to follow a superintendent's directives, the real power lies elsewhere. If other elected officials are overly critical of a superintendent and see their job as holding them accountable, it can create a negative tone throughout the community. And if powerful and connected community members are seen as always getting their way, it can affect a school system's culture. Superintendents must, of course, work closely with and engage the community. After all, they are the stewards of the community's values as manifest through the election of a board of education. Yet, system leaders must be attentive to the impact these dynamics have on the culture of the district and act accordingly.

CHANGE MANAGEMENT

One important aspect of the superintendency is about change management, and that requires vision and innovation. For too long, change management efforts have been in response to low standardized test scores and decreasing fiscal resources. These are real issues that cannot be discounted. But communities want something more. Students, families, communities, and employees have the right to know how efforts to increase scores serve a larger vision. What will students achieve if they pass state tests? What will they lose out on by focusing too much on the state test? Will passing state mandated tests lead to better opportunities post-graduation and what does it mean for a community? Superintendents must be able to answer these questions and organize a transformation effort around the answer. That effort requires innovation, which is extremely complex given the tractor beam of the status quo in some school systems. Bureaucracy has been calcified in public education through layers of bureaucratic policy; hence, a superintendent needs to find ways to adapt and push in the service of their vision.

An innovation strategy rests on a few key principles, with the most important one being that the superintendent must spend as much time as possible leading and letting others manage. This balance can be difficult in smaller districts, as the superintendent often plays multiple roles. Yet and still, the superintendent reflects on a regular basis, "What's the work that only I can do?" If a superintendent finds he or she is doing work that someone else can do, the work needs to be reassigned to that person or taught to someone. When leaders spend time doing work that someone else can do, they take time away from their most important work, which is leading a community through a transformation process.

Transparency of information is another key principle of innovation strategies. In this day and age, everyone either already knows what's happening, has heard rumors of what's going on, or will eventually learn the truth. Superintendents must constantly guard against rumor control in the face of social media. The results from the 2020 survey showed that superintendents invested in social media, whether through their own profiles or a district operation. It is essential that such investments are geared toward proactive messaging, transparency, and rumor control. Given the decline in local media, superintendents must double down on efforts to inform internal and external communities about what's happening throughout the system and why. It is only through such transparency that superintendents can build trust. That trust is essential for leaders to grow a volunteer army that will help them accelerate change.

Jon Kotter (*Harvard Business Review*, November 2012) writes about the need for leaders to have a volunteer army. Essentially, it is a diverse group of people who are eager to help the leader design and execute a transformation strategy. Volunteer armies are comprised of people from throughout the system who can be activated to bring their knowledge and experience to bear on the problem at hand. Since those who are closest to the problem are best suited for solving it, they need to be given permission and opportunity to try out bold new practices. In order to activate a volunteer army, superintendents need to run what Kotter refers to as a "dual operating system." Such systems ensure that regular operations run smoothly, while also seeding innovation by activating the volunteer army.

Let's say the district wants to open access to advanced courses in a high school and believes that "flipping" classes will lead to improvements in teaching and learning. Simply creating a policy and requiring it does not account for all the issues that educators may confront, such as teacher and counselor beliefs about students, teacher readiness to support and differentiate, parental skepticism, and student readiness. An alternative approach is to have ready and willing teachers begin the process, work out the kinks, and then make their learning and practice public for other teachers to learn from. This is not a pilot—in fact, there are few, if any, true pilots in public schools—rather, it's a staggered implementation that allows for the kinks to be worked out in service of better practices. This kind of dual operating system allows for a leader to be strategic and attend to all the various considerations that may arise. More importantly, it enables quick action, as a volunteer army can immediately start innovating and implementing a change, which is essential in today's fast-moving world.

CONCLUSION

Ultimately, the superintendent's job is to remove barriers to success. Leaders can always find reasons *not* to change: underperforming schools that families don't want to send their children to, gates established by adults that limit opportunities for children, or lack of incentives to innovate. This is no longer sufficient for our children today, as the transitions in our society demand new approaches. Superintendents cannot just stand on the top of a hill and demand new approaches and different results. They have to lead—sometimes by pushing and sometimes by pulling—their teams, employees, and the entire community to charge the hill with them. As the 2020 decennial survey shows, the job of a superintendent is a complex one, with myriad challenges and opportunities. It can also be one with moments of joy and true accomplishment and satisfaction. As superintendents organize transformation efforts grounded in continuous improvement, equity, and learning, it is essential that they embrace the complexity of change in order to serve all our children at a higher level than ever before.

REFERENCES

Cilluffo, A., and Cohn, D. (2019, April 11). "6 Demographic Trends Shaping the U.S. and the World in 2019." *Fact Tank News in the Numbers*. Pew Research Trust. Retrieved from https://www.pewresearch.org/fact-tank/2019/04/11/6-demographic-trends-shaping-the-u-s-and-the-world-in-2019/.

Hutchings, G. C., Jr., and Brown, J. L. (2020). "Chapter 5: The Current Work of the American Superintendent." In C. Tienken (Ed.), *The American Superintendent 2020 Decennial Study*. Lanham, MD: Rowman & Littlefield.

Kotter, J. P. (2012, Nov). Accelerate! *Harvard Business Review* 90 (11), 45–58.

Laloggia, J. (2019, May 15). "6 Facts about U.S. Political Independents." *Fact Tank News in the Numbers*. Pew Research Trust. Retrieved from https://www.pewresearch.org/fact-tank/2019/05/15/facts-about-us-political-independents/.

Pew Research Trust. (2017). "The Partisan Divides over Political Values Widen." Author. Retrieved from https://www.people-press.org/2017/10/05/1-partisan-divides-over-political-values-widen/.

Index

About the Editor and Contributors

John L. Brown (PhD) is a researcher-in-residence at AASA. Previously, he served as executive director of curriculum and instruction for Alexandria City Public Schools, director of staff development for Prince George's County Public Schools, and consultant and staff writer for ASCD. He is the coauthor with Dan Domenech and Mort Sherman of *Personalizing 21st Century Education: A Framework for Student Success* (2016).

Salih Cevik is a PhD candidate and graduate assistant in educational administration and policy at the University of Georgia. He obtained his master of arts degree in educational leadership and policy at the University of Minnesota and is the recipient of the Turkish Study Abroad Scholarship, CEHD Advanced Study Scholarship, and the Ray E. Bruce Award.

Mary Lynne Derrington (EdD) is an associate professor of educational leadership and policy studies at the University of Tennessee. She teaches courses in leadership, supervision, and policy. She has written widely about educational administration, school and district leadership, and teacher evaluation. Before entering higher education, Dr. Derrington served for eighteen years as a Washington State superintendent.

Margaret Grogan (PhD) is professor of educational leadership and policy at the Attalah College of Educational Studies, Chapman University, California. She graduated from Washington State University with a PhD in educational administration. She has published many articles and chapters and has authored, coauthored, or edited six books. She is the specialty chief editor for the leadership in education section of the journal *Frontiers in Education*. Her current research focuses on women in leadership, gender and education, the moral and ethical dimensions of leadership, and leadership for social justice.

Sonya Douglass Horsford (EdD) is associate professor of education leadership in the Department of Organization and Leadership at Teachers College, Columbia University, where she also serves as codirector of the Urban Education Leaders Program—a doctoral program for aspiring urban school superintendents. Her research focuses on the politics of race, education policy, and urban school leadership.

Gregory C. Hutchings Jr. (EdD) is the superintendent of Alexandria City Public Schools. He served as a teacher, assistant principal, and middle school principal before becoming superintendent of Shaker Heights Schools in Cleveland, Ohio, in 2013. In 2009, he was named Tennessee Middle School Principal of the Year. Dr. Hutchings holds a doctorate from the College of William and Mary.

Meredith Mountford (PhD) is an associate professor at Florida Atlantic University in the Department of Educational Leadership and Research Methodology. She is also the director of the UCEA Center for Research on District Governance as well as past-president of AERA's Research on the Superintendency. Dr. Mountford researches school boards, superintendents, educational policy, and gender.

Angel Miles Nash (PhD) is an assistant professor of leadership development at Chapman University in the Attallah College of Educational Studies. Angel earned her PhD in educational administration and supervision from the University of Virginia. She taught and led in K–12 schools in Washington, DC, California, and Virginia, which galvanized her research examining the intersectional realities of girls and women.

George J. Petersen (PhD) has been a public school teacher, administrator, and university faculty member. Currently, he is the founding dean of Clemson University's College of Education. Petersen is the author or coauthor of three books and over one hundred book chapters, professional articles, research papers, and commissioned reports. Much of his scholarly work has focused on the executive leadership of district superintendents. Petersen's research has been widely published and is internationally recognized for its quality and impact.

Jayson W. Richardson (PhD) is an associate professor in the Department of Educational Leadership Studies at the University of Kentucky. His research passion centers on understanding leadership within innovative school models with a focus on school technology leadership. He is a director of the UCEA Center for the Advanced Study of Technology Leadership in Education (CASTLE).

Wendy Y. Robinson (EdD) has served as superintendent of Fort Wayne (Indiana) Community Schools since July 2003. In nearly five decades with FWCS, she has served as a teacher, principal, deputy superintendent, and superintendent. Dr. Robinson has degrees from DePauw University, Indiana University, Indiana University-Purdue University Fort Wayne, and Ball State University, where she obtained her EdD in educational administration and supervision.

Joshua P. Starr (EdD) is the chief executive officer (CEO) of PDK International. Prior to joining PDK, Starr served as superintendent in Stamford, Connecticut, and Montgomery County Public Schools, Maryland. As CEO, Dr. Starr has brought innovation to the organization and led the diversification of programming while building on PDK's 110+ years legacy. Under Starr's leadership, PDK has expanded the reach of Educators Rising, launched Educators Rising Collegiate, increased foundation support, greatly expanded the online presence of Kappan magazine, created networks and services for school system leaders, and renewed support for PDK members.

Christopher H. Tienken (EdD) is an associate professor of Education Leadership, Management, and Policy at Seton Hall University. Tienken's research interests include curriculum and assessment policy at the state, national, and international levels. He has been a visiting professor at the Università degli Studi Roma Tre, Rome, Italy, and the Università di Catania, Sicily, Italy, where he has ongoing research projects. Tienken served as an assistant superintendent, middle school principal, assistant principal, and teacher before entering higher education.

David G. Title (EdD) is an assistant clinical professor of educational leadership at Sacred Heart University in Fairfield, Connecticut. He is the director of the superintendent of schools certification and EdD programs at Sacred Heart. Dr. Title spent thirty-seven years in public education, the last fourteen as a superintendent of schools in Bloomfield, Connecticut (eight years) and Fairfield, Connecticut (six years).

Sevda Yildirim is a PhD candidate and graduate assistant in educational administration and policy at the University of Georgia. Her research interests are teacher evaluation and supervision practices and policies, and implementation of professional development. Prior to coming to the University of Georgia, she earned a master's degree in educational leadership at the University of Florida.

Sally J. Zepeda (PhD) is a professor of educational administration and policy at the University of Georgia. She teaches courses in leadership, supervision, professional learning, and personnel evaluation. She has written widely about school and district leadership, succession planning, and teacher and leader supervision and evaluation. Before entering higher education, Dr. Zepeda served as a building-level leader and teacher.